Dr. Augustine U. S. Obaje

Biblical Requirements for Preaching: Hermeneutical Reflect for Africa

Dr. Augustine U. S. Obaje

Biblical Requirements for Preaching: Hermeneutical Reflect for Africa

The current adulterated Preaching situation in many of our African Churches is a thing of concern for a Biblical mind

Blessed Hope Publishing

Imprint
Any brand names and product names mentioned in this book are subject to trademark, brand or patent protection and are trademarks or registered trademarks of their respective holders. The use of brand names, product names, common names, trade names, product descriptions etc. even without a particular marking in this work is in no way to be construed to mean that such names may be regarded as unrestricted in respect of trademark and brand protection legislation and could thus be used by anyone.

Cover image: www.ingimage.com

Publisher:
Blessed Hope Publishing
is a trademark of
Dodo Books Indian Ocean Ltd. and OmniScriptum S.R.L publishing group

120 High Road, East Finchley, London, N2 9ED, United Kingdom
Str. Armeneasca 28/1, office 1, Chisinau MD-2012, Republic of Moldova, Europe
Printed at: see last page
ISBN: 978-620-4-18829-4

DEDICATION

This work is dedicated to God and my wife Sarah Augustine Obaje.

ACKNOWLEDGEMENTS

I acknowledge God for giving me the wisdom and grace to complete this study. I am indebted to my supervisor, Dr. Ige, S. Abiodun for guiding me through the writing of this research. I thank Dr. Okpe Nicholas for always encouraging me through his kind words. Also to professor Enegho, who relentlessly taught me Research which has greatly assisted in this work? To my HOD, Dr. Akoh I.Y for his academic critical eyes in all of the defence.

I am eternally grateful to my wife (my heart) Sarah Augustine Obaje and all our children: Jill, Jemaimah, and Bethany who prayed and supported daddy in the process of the thesis. My wife and friend, you have continued to remain a virtuous woman despite the various storms that came our way in order to stop the school. She supported me so much in all areas; she is blessed of the Lord. I thank my children for their patience throughout the studies.

My profound gratitude goes all the Religious Department lecturers. May God bless you all? My special thanks to the entire Post-Graduate School, faculty and staff for being part of my life at the University. What could I have achieved without my colleagues and school mates motivation thank you all.

TABLE OF CONTENTS

DEDICATION- - -   - - - - - - - - - - 1

ACKNOWLEDGEMENT- -   - - - - - - - - - 1

TABLE OF CONTENTS- - - - - - - - - - - - - - - - 1

ABSTRACT- -3

CHAPTER ONE: INTRODUCTION

1.1 Background to the Problem- - - - - - - - - - - - - -4

1.2 Statement of the Problem- - - - - - - - - - - - - -7

1.3 Aim and Objectives of the Study- - - - - - - - - - 8

1.4 Justification for the Study- - - - - - - - - - - - - -8

1.5 Scope and Limitation of the Study- - - - - - - - - - - 9

1.6 Research Methodology- - - - - - - - - - - - - - - -9

1.7 Organisation of the Study- - - - - - - - - - - - - -9

2. **CHAPTER TWO: LITERATURE REVIEW**

2.1 The Concept of Preaching from Biblical Perspective- - - - - 10

2.2 Old Testament Concept of Preaching- - - - - - - - - - -11

2.3 New Testament Concept of Preaching- - - - - - - - - -15

2.4 Preaching in the Early Church- - - - - - - - - - - - -16

3. **CHAPTER THREE: SOCIO-HISTORICAL BACKGROUND AND EXEGESIS OF 2 TIMOTHY**

3.1 Introduction- - - - - - - - - - - - - - - - - - - -18

3.2 About the Book of 2 Timothy - - - - - - - - - - - - - 19

3.3 The Charge to Preach the Word: 2 Timothy 4:1-2 - - - - - - 21

3.4 The Reason for the Charge 2 Timothy 4:3-5- - - - - - - - - - 34

3.5 Conclusion - - - - - - 36

4.   CHAPTER FOUR: THE RELEVANCE OF 2 TIMOTHY 4:1-5, TO

THE CONTEMPORARY NIGERIAN CHURCH

4.1   The Need to Preach the Word in the Context of the Nigerian Church-   37

4.2   The Nature of Preaching in the Contemporary Nigerian Church-   -   40

4.3   The Effects and Implications of Preaching in the Contemporary Nigerian

         Church- - -   - 44

4.4   The Implication of not preaching the Word- - -   - - -   - -   - 47

5.   CHAPTER FIVE: SUMMARYAND CONCLUSION

5.1   Summary- -   - - - - - - - - - - - - - - -   - - -   -50

5.2   Conclusion- -   - - - - - - - - - - - - -   - -   - 50

5.3   Recommendations- -   - - - - - - - - - - - -   - -   - 51

         WORKS CITED -   - - - - - - - - - - - - - -   - - - 53

ABSTRACT

The current situation in contemporary Nigerian Churches is something of great concern, issues where one observes prophetic and healing "gymnastics" replacing the ministry of the word. This type of situation suggests that it is almost impossible to differentiate when God is speaking and when human self is at play. In pursuit of self glory and personal interest by some of these contemporary preachers, sound biblical preaching and teaching that address all aspects of life seems to be missing. The latter presumably is the cause of extreme prosperity preaching, healing and deliverance, and miracles which have become the order of the day on media and in various places of Christian gatherings. It is observed that great majority of people prefer to rush to these places of worship where rebuke and correction is lacking from the Pulpit. In situating this problem, the research reckon not only with the biblical charge from Paul to Timothy, but also with current preaching, teaching and correction issues in our Nigerian Churches.

The research uses exegetical and socio-historical method to examine the background that led to Paul's charge to Timothy. The exegetical method is to study the text in its original Greek language. The adopted method will help both the researcher and the readers to get acquainted with the contextual situation of the text. The socio-historical method study's the social context for which the text emerged. At least, the method could enable the reader to see the incompatibility of Paul's charge to timothy in connection to some Church preaching ministry in Nigeria.

CHAPTER ONE

INTRODUCTION

1.1   Background to the Study

It is observed that the contemporary religious gymnastics in Nigerian Churches has become so endemic in the body of Christ. It seems to be affecting the spirituality of so many who profess themselves as Christians. This could be the root cause of much immorality going on in our society today. Biblical sound preaching and teaching ministrytoday seem to have become something of a mirage as against the thought of Paul in 2 Timothy 4:1-5,Paul stressed his concern for preaching in verse 2, the word in its original form goes thus:

Κηρύσσω ὀ λόγοςἐφίστημιευκαίρως ἀκαίρωςελέγχω ἐπιτιμάω παρακαλέωεν πᾶς μακροθυμία καί διδαχή (2Tim 4:2). The English translation is, Preach the word, be instant in season, out of season, reprove, rebuke, exhort with all longsuffering and doctrine (2Tim 4:2)

Biblical sound preaching and teaching ministry today have been replaced with extremes like, prophecy, healing, deliverance, anointing, breakthrough and die by fire syndrome. We live a time that many preachers and their followers are doing what seems right in their own eyes neglecting the sound preaching of the word, a generation that Preachers preach selfish interest instead of preaching the word. They attract people to themselves instead of directing them to God and to the truth of His word. In other words, they preach more of themselves and less of God's word. Femi Bitrus Adeleye observes that: "These are times when sin is being redefined so that the things that used to be sin are no longer considered sinful...these are days of confusion in which the doors of the church are wide open to worldly values and standards" (6).

It is clear that there is need for sound biblical preaching and teaching of God's word for the Church to be spiritually strong and healthy. By that, the strange wind of all kinds of false teachings will not be able to penetrate as against God's standard for God's people. There is also the need for preachers to examine themselves and have a rethink of the ministry of preaching and teaching which they claim they have been called into. Looking at what is happening in this present age, George E. Janvier quoted. Samuel W. Kunhiyop saying:

You are going out in the midst of false prophets and wrong doctrines, but you must come out on top, preaching the word. Remember my advice to you. Three things you are required to do in ministry. Number one,which is important, preach the word. Number two which is more important, preach the word. Number three which is the most important of all; preach the word (7).

The emphasis on the charge to preach the word which might be appealing to the conscience of any serious and true preacher of the word shows how true preaching of the word will go a long way in combating false teachings and wrong doctrines. This will also enable many Church members to distinguish between sound teachings of the word of God from false teachings and wrong doctrines. Most especially those who desire to have preachers and prophets who would tell them "thus says the Lord," before they would believe what is been preached. It will also enhance healthy spiritual growth of the Church which John Stott pointed out, "If the Church is to flourish again, there is need for faithful, powerful, biblical preaching. God still urges His people to listen, and His preachers to proclaim His word" (21). The Church of God cannot grow without sound and faithful biblical preaching which should be given a top priority.

For the evangelical denominations, we profess to be committed first and foremost to the proclamation and preservation of the Gospel. Yet it is worth asking ourselves afresh if the Gospel truly has grasped our hearts and lives. Indeed, that is the essence of being a Christian. Whether we find ourselves discouraged by failure or elated by success, we must again and again grasp the word of the Law and the word of the Gospel in their distinction from one another. This distinction is not a truth which may quietly rest in an outline of systematic theology, but bears fundamental hermeneutical implications. Through this distinction the Bible offers its own interpretation, and does not remain merely a book that I read, but is "the book that reads me."

Beginning with the Old Testament through to the New, God is usually found speaking. He spoke in the Old Testament days; He spoke while the Lord Jesus was on earth; and He continues to speak in the New Testament church. We learn from the Bible that God has a prime work to perform on earth, which is, to utter His own word. If the word of God is taken away, then almost nothing is left of God's work. No word, no work. When the word is eliminated, the work is reduced to nearly zero. We must therefore recognize the place of God's word in His work. Once the word is removed the work of God ceases immediately, for God operates through His word; He treats His word as His work. The work of God is filled with His words.

If anyone teaches false doctrines and does not agree to the sound instruction of our Lord Jesus Christ and to godly teaching, he is conceited and understands nothing. He has an unhealthy interest in controversies and quarrels about words that result in envy, strife, malicious talk, evil suspicions and constant friction between men of corrupt mind, who have been robbed of the truth and who think that godliness is a means to financial gain (NIV) 1 Tim 6:3-5.

Paul's letters to Timothy and Titus are often referred to as the Pastoral Epistles. These letters are unique in the Pauline corpus. They are personal letters from Paul, like Philemon, which are written to individuals instead of churches. However, these letters are unique in that Titus and Timothy were Paul's associates in the ministry. Paul often involved these two workers in churches he had founded or those in which he was actively involved. For example, Timothy helped Paul establish churches at Philippi, Thessalonica, and Berea (Acts 16:1–17:14). Six of Paul's epistles to churches mentioned Timothy in the greetings.

 Tradition holds that Timothy remained a leader at the church of Ephesus following Paul's death and was eventually martyred for his faith. In the Pastoral Epistles, Paul addressed a vast array of ministerial issues, such as the qualifications of a minister, practical wisdom on how a minister should approach a task, and how a minister should use the Word of God. Second Timothy bears a certain amount of urgency as this letter appears to be the last letter Paul wrote during his imprisonment in Rome. It is clear from his tone; Paul was involved in a compassionate correspondence with someone he regarded as a son (II Timothy 1:2). In the midst of this letter, Paul gives the reader fundamental wisdom regarding ministry, in particular, pastoral ministry. To read this letter as a dry discourse on pastoral ministry would be artificial and take away from the weight of the occasion.

The passage above reveals who a preacher of the gospel is and how he or she occupies a central place in the life of a congregation. The nature of his work enables him to be called first and foremost a theologian. He is an interpreter and his theological interpretation of a particular passage is the fruit of the reflection of the church on the truth revealed in the word of God which may be modified by the knowledge of a theological truth based on other passages. It is the knowledge of theology that develops our mind in the image of God, knows and appreciates God's revelation, knows God better, arranges doctrine for Christian fellowship, recognizes heresy and used in popular instruction in any Christian gathering. This is because the subject and object of theology is God. The scope of theology includes not only God, but creation, human being, the fall, redemption, final destiny among others. Sound biblical theology therefore provides support, shape and stability to the body of Christ. Surprisingly, the church is divided into two: the part that has correct understanding of what theology means and the part that gets 'threatened' at the mere mention of theology and feels it has not gotten a space in the church. The objective of this paper, therefore, is to examine the importance of rightly dividing the Word of Truth Ορθοτομουντα τον λογον της αληθειας, and to re-establish its theological implication for today's church.

1.2   Statement of the Problem

The current situation in contemporary Nigerian Churches is something of great concern, issues where one observes prophetic and healing gymnastics replacing the ministry of the word. This type of situation suggests that it is almost impossible to differentiate when God is speaking and when human self is at play. In pursuit of self glory and personal interest by some of these contemporary preachers, sound biblical preaching and teaching that address all aspects of life seemsto be missing. The latter presumably is the cause of extreme prosperity preaching, healing and deliverance, and miracles which have become the order of the day on media and in various places of Christian gatherings. It is observed that great majority of people prefer to rush to these places of worship where rebuke and correction is lacking from the Pulpit.

In situating this problem, the research reckon not only with the biblical charge from Paul to Timothy, but also with current preaching, teaching and correction issues in our Nigerian Churches. As a result ofthese happenings in the Church today, many Ministers prefer to preach what the majority like to hear. These current happenings are the reasons the researcher deems it fit to research and make exegetical analysis of the charge to preach the word in 2 Timothy 4: 1-5 and its relevance for the contemporary Nigerian Church.

1.3   Aim and Objectives of the Study

The study seeks to inquire into the relevance of 2Timothy 4:1-5 on the contemporary Nigerian Churches. The aim is to find out if the contemporary Nigerian Churches and their leadership are actually being faithful in preaching and teaching the word of God as counseled by Paul to young Timothy. The aim is hoped to be achieved through the following objectives:

1.   to alert and encourage the preaching of the word of God to be taken with all seriousness by those who are saddled with the responsibility no matter the challenges of the time,

2.   to encourage preachers and teachers of the word of God to be diligent students of the Bible, for sound teaching, appropriate application and godly living,

3.   to encourage preachers and teachers to be more faithful in preaching the word of God,

4.   to present and defend the values of Paul's charge to Timothy, regarding the preaching of the word of God,

5.   topresent the effects of the charge to preach the word of Godon the health of the church.

1.4   Justification for the Study

The study is an ambitious research. It is determined to lay bare biblical trends and importance of preaching God's word as counseled by Paul to Timothy. Arguably, the topic is rarely sighted in recent academic journals. This attempt therefore, is structured to motivate preachers to engage meaningful, theological, and homiletical preaching in the Churches. The study is hoped to be helpful to young undergraduate pastors coming into full time ministry. To the graduate and post graduates, the research lends itself to further inquiry and analysis of pastoral responsibility in terms of preaching the word. The study seeks to achieve an academic and theological interpretation so as to give a better understanding to preachers of the gospel in the Nigerian Churches to have a morally upright and an egalitarian Nigerian society.

1.5   Scope and Limitation of the Study

The charge to preach the word of God is encouraged in different passages, both Old Testament and New Testament. This research therefore cannot lay claim in covering all arrears that talk about preaching the word. As such, there search is an attempt to inquire and analyze2 Timothy 4:1-5 as well as making reference to some relevant passages in the Scripture and following the topic under consideration.

1.6   Research Methodology

The research will be library based. It uses exegetical and socio-historical method to examine the background that led to Paul's charge to Timothy. The exegetical method is to study the text in its original Greek language. The method adopted in this research will help both the researcher and the readers to get acquainted with the contextual situation of the text. The socio-historical method study's the social context for which the text emerged.

1.7   Organization of Work

        Chapter one introduces the research topic under consideration: "The charge to preach the word in 2 Timothy 4:1-5 and its implications on the Nigerian Churches." Most importantly, the background to the problem, statement of the problem, aim and objective of the study, justification for the study, scope and limitation, and research methodology have been stated and discussed for easy understanding of the study.

CHAPTER TWO

2.0   LITERATURE REVIEW

The Concept of Preaching from Biblical Perspective

Down through the ages, if there is any means, by which God has been communicating to His people, in order to encourage, rebuke, correct, and warn them, He usually use His word. The word of God usually comes with power and authority through the instrument which He chooses to pass His message across. God's people on the other hand, are often left with the choice of accepting or rejecting what God tells them, but His word has never failed to accomplish the purpose which it is meant for (Isa 55:10-11). John R. W. Stott affirms that, "God still speaks through what He has spoken, and that nothing is more necessary for the life, growth, and health of Churches or of Christians than they should hear and heed to what the Spirit is saying to them through His ancient, yet ever modern-word" (5).

To have a good grasp of what this ancient word of God has done in the lives of many generations ago, and is still doing even in this present age, the researcher deems it fit to consult the works of scholars who have written relevant materials on the subject matter, as this chapter focuses on the concept of preaching during the Old and the New Testaments periods. The ministry of preaching the word of God during the early Church will be taken into consideration also. This will certainly pave a way and provide the ground for doing the analysis of the text for this research in chapter three to see how it can benefit the contemporary Church that is already facing a lot of challenges from within and outside, due to unknown reasons or   ignorance, and possibly due to negligence of sound preaching and teaching of God's word by many preachers and teachers of the word who have been entrusted with the responsibility.

God loves and cares for His creation especially man whom He has created in His own image and likeness and for His own glory and pleasure. Right from the fall of man God has been in the business of seeking to reconcile mankind back to Him, by using different means in various occasions to communicate to His people.

The following is just a highlight of few of those instances during the Old Testament period where God communicated His word to His people the way He chose or wanted.

During the patriarchal period when God first and foremost singled out Abram (Gen 12:1-3), whose name was eventually changed to Abraham (Gen 17:5), God himself communicated directly to Abraham, the man whom He has chosento walk with as a means of demonstrating and revealing His plan of salvation to mankind, following the fall of man.

Looking at the history of Abraham and his descendants, it is from this chosen race that the idea of priests and prophets who served as God's instruments came about. Those were people whom God used as a means of getting His message across.

Now,howdid God speak through these people? What often constitute God's message to His People? How were they delivering the messages given to them? What often was the response of the People then? To answer these questions, it is unwise to take for granted the offices of priests and prophets during the Old Testament dispensation.

Priests

In Exodus 29:44-45, the Lord declares, "I will consecrate...Aaron and his sons to serve as priests. Then I will dwell among the Israelites and be their God." It is very obvious here that the issue of priesthood was God's idea. Priests were appointed to render service to God and to His people, and the Lord had promised them His presence. To serve as priests was a great privilege which ZacPoonen says, "it is a tremendous privilege to be called by God to serve Him. But it brings with it a great and awesome responsibility too" (3). The work of priests was so demanding and required diligence and discipline in all aspects as they make voluntary offerings in communion with God as acts of devotion or consecration with praise, as well as occasional sacrifices for some certain sins and defilements.

The priests usually make pronouncementof blessings to and for the people using the model high priestly prayer of Numbers 6:24-27 which was usually recited to bless worshippers with the assurance of God's acceptance. The work of priests was indeed an enormous task and sensitive, as such Singer highlights some characteristics of the priests' lives and ministries which provide a better understanding of what priests were, and the nature of their work. These characteristics of priests' life and ministry comprise the following as stated by Dwight Singer:

1.   They were chosen by God and distinguished from the majority of other Israelites.

2.   They were consecrated to office in a public ceremony that distinguished them for service.

3.   They had a higher standard for life and conduct and service than the common worshipper.

4.   They were provided for by the gifts and offerings that were brought to the temple, but their duty was to wave them before the Lord to demonstrate that they were His.

5.   Their primary responsibility was to officiate at the Temple.

6.   They were to make intercessory prayer for the People (Num 6:23-27).

7.   They were to teach the Law (Lev 10:9-11;Deut 17:9-11)

8.   They had no secret society in contrast to the secret societies of pagan priests.

9.   They were to maintain the vessels of the Temple, the lights, the bread, and the fire.

10.   The high Priest had the privilege of entering the presence of the glory of God in the Holy of Holies once a year, on the Day of Atonement (8).

It is a serious thing to be a servant of God whether a priest, a teacher, and preacher of His word. God is usually strict with anyone whom He has chosen to do His work,aspunishment often follows any violation of His rules. For instance, in Leviticus 10:1and2 "Aaron's sons Nadab and Abihu took their censers, put fire in them and added incense; and they offered unauthorized fire before the Lord contrary to His command. So fire came out from the presence of the Lord and consumed them, and they died before the Lord".

Another practical example is found in 2 Samuel 6:1-8. David, when he became king, he modified God's commands. David was taking the ark back to Jerusalem which was a good thing, but he did not do it the way God has commanded in the Law. God has commanded the Levite to carry the ark on their shoulders. But David modified that command and placed the ark on cart. He was imitating the Philistines who had adopted that method a few years earlier. As the oxen carried the ark they stumbled. When Uzzah saw that, he reached out his hand and held the ark to prevent it from falling. And God killed Uzzah immediately "for his irreverence" (v.7).

When God's shepherds make a mistake, the sheep suffer too. David had made a mistake and Uzzah suffered for it. If the same thing happens to the contemporary Church where so many so called "Men of God" preach wrong doctrines which often lead to wrong application and wrong living, imagine how many of the Church members will have to suffer the consequences. The work of God must be taking with all seriousnessandconsciousness by those who have been saddled with the responsibility of either administration, preaching, and teaching without violating the laid down rules in the Scripture.

Prophets

Prophets were also instruments that Yahweh used in the Old Testament to convey His message to His People. To discuss their role or their proper function in Israel's social, political, and religious life, in order to have a glimpse of the concept of Old Testament preaching, Charles T Beattie says:

there is...a recognition or wide consensus that much of what the Prophets spoke was not foretelling, that is they spoke God's Word regarding their immediate historical context and the situation they lived in rather than distant future...it is also helpful to recognize that a prophecy can be both foretelling and forth telling at the same time... In the Old Testament, prophecy can also be applied to Christ or end time...prophecy might be unconditional, stating what will certainly happen, while another might be conditional, saying what the consequences of certain actions will be if they are carried out, or pronouncing the judgment that will be passed unless the People repent (3).

Prophets were used by God during the Old Testament to declare either God's message of encouragement to His People in difficult times or message of warning and judgment whenever God's People persist in doing evil. They were also used to predict what will happen in the future.

Regarding their identity and position, Beattie further observes that: "there are a wide range of suggestions for different positions...they were an official group linked to the temple, they held official positions in the royal court as advisers of the king. They were social reformers, God's messengers, God's representatives and ambassadors. They were radicals on the fringes of society" (2013:3).

In regard to what Beattie says, it is obvious that during the Old Testament period prophets served as God's mouthpiece in the temple, in the palace, and in the society at large. They played vital roles as God's messengers and representatives in bringing transformation in the lives of people, and warning them against any form of disobedience and ungodliness which was often accompanied by God's divine punishment. In like manner, Jean Calvin stresses that: "A prophet comes in the name of the Lord, directed by the Spirit of God; and deliver to men the pure doctrines which he receives from heaven" (250).

God's message through the prophets He uses as His mouthpiece, mostly aims at addressing the spiritual condition of the people which geared toward pure and holy living, God's punishment on sin and restoration. Sometimes God's word is opposed and rejected, in fact not only the message but even the messenger's life becomes at stake. Considering some few practical examples of the prophets of God in the Scripture and the roles they played is very crucial to this work.

Elijah was a prophet chosen and directed by the word of Yahweh. During the reign of King Ahab, it is clear that Elijah was involved in the palace affairs. He brings messages of judgment to King Ahab (1 Kgs 17:1; 19:15-18). God used him to bring back to life the child oftheZarephath widow who said to him "now I know for sure that you are a man of God and that Yahweh truly speaks through you". Elijah, like other prophets was a man of God and God's mouthpiece that brought comfort to this woman, message of judgment toKing Ahab and the like.

Micaiah was a very honest and courageous prophet unlike other prophets who told Ahab what he wanted to hear. But Micaiah says "as surely as Yahweh lives, I will say only what Yahweh tells me to say."Micaiahdeclared that it was a lying spirit that inspired the other Prophets to tell Ahab he would be successful in battle in order to lead him to his death. One of them rebuked Micaiah and Ahab hadMicaiah arrested. Ahab hatedMicaiah because he never prophesies anything good about him (1 Kgs 22:1-8, 14-26 NIV).

These are few of the Old Testament prophets whom Yahweh spoke through and used,to accomplish His purpose. They played very significant roles during those periods. Prophets who were called by God actually "preserved the teaching and practices of righteousness, and Yahweh's way among His people for the blessing of the nations, by faithfully passing on the word given by God… under the inspiration of the Holy Spirit" (Beattie, 2013:10). But for the fact that there were prophets who were called by God, used by Him, and who faithfully carried on His mission and purposes, there were also false prophets who did otherwise (Ezek 34:1ff). Like the present day so called men of God, which chapter four is going to address in line with the relevance of the study to the contemporary preachers of the word, following the analysis of the charge to preach the word in 2Timothy 4:1-5, the text under consideration where the topic emanated.

New Testament Concept of Preaching

As it has been sated earlier, the writer of the Book of Hebrews says: "In the past God spoke to our forefathers through the prophets at many times and in various ways, but in these last days He has spoken to us by His Son, whom He appointed heir of all things, and through whom He made the Universe." (Heb 1:1, 2 NIV). When Jesus came, His message was very simple like John the Baptist who preceded Him. Both preached that "the kingdom of God is at hand" and that men could enter it through repentance and belief in the gospel (Mark1:14-15; Matt 3:1-12 NIV).

 The gospel that both Jesus and John preached during their ministry here on earth according to Harry R. Boer, "...is the joyful news that God forgives those who repent, and He receives them as His children. At the same time, the preaching of Jesus was not an entirely a new message. It aroseoutof and continued at adeeper level from the message of the Old Testament..." (15).This shows that Jesus' message during His ministry here on earth was built on the teachings of the Old Testament and many prophecies were directly about Him, which found their fulfillment in Him.

The message of the gospel in the New Testament which originated from the Old Testament centers on Christ. In other words, Christ is the central message of both the Old and the New Testaments, which focuses on God's redemptive work of salvation for mankind. Jesus Christ is the good news that has been preachedby the Apostles and still being proclaimed today. Apostle Paul challenges and admonishes the Galatians as he declares:

I am astonished that you are so quickly deserting the one who called you by the grace of Christ and turning to a different gospel which is really no gospel at all. Evidently some people are throwing you into confusion and are trying to pervert the gospel of Christ. But even if we or an angel from heaven should preach a gospel other than the one we preach to you, let him be eternally condemned (Gal 1:6-8NIV).

 God's messenger,who proclaims His word, delivers only the message he receives from God,likeApostle Paul and many Old Testament priests and prophets who preceded him, as it has been highlighted and briefly discussed above.

Preachers and teachers, who are called by God, preach and teach God's wordfaithfully,nothing less nothing more. The aim is to bring about transformation in the lives of people by the power of the Holy Spirit. They present everyone complete in Christ and inspire believers to greater faith and service to God. In the words of Warren W. Wiersbeas quoted by Janvier, "preaching develops the mind, brings spiritual transformation, and challenges Christians to action. The action may be a decision for Christ, a decision for change, or a decision for ministry" (15). This is the goal and purpose of the New Testament preaching, for healthy spiritual growth, for building healthy Churches and society.

For more understanding of the New Testament concept of preaching, Apostle Paul says: "...we preach Christ crucified..." (1Cor 1:23NIV), the source and purpose of preaching to any serious preacher and teacher of God's word, which John Piper in a form of an outline states:

1.   The Goal of preaching: the Glory of God

2.   The Ground of preaching: the Cross of Christ

3.   The Gift of preaching: the power of the Holy Spirit (19).

Piper goes further to quote James Stewart a Scottish Preacher who said, "The aims of allgenuine preaching are to quicken the conscience by the holiness of God, to open theheart to the love of God, to devote the will to the purpose of God" (19).

The concept of New Testament preaching can be fully understood, following what Piper and Stewart said, because any preaching that does not aim at glorifying God and making the cross of Christ the center, through the power of the Holy Spirit is a different gospel. God's word if it is sincerely preached or taught restores the holiness and the righteousness of God in man through faith in Christ Jesus.

The Concept of Preaching in the Early Church

The Church as the body of believers began in Jerusalem. At the Jewish feast of Pentecost, seven weeks after the crucifixion of Jesus Christ as a result of the preaching of Peter. The Church in the beginning had a good number of People as its members and as a community. The Church lived a life of fellowship, worship, and a mutual help, receiving new members daily (Acts 2:43-47 NIV). During this period, the message of the Church regarding the preaching of the word wassimple: repentance from sin, the death and resurrection of Christ, with strong emphasis on Christ's resurrection and baptism (Acts 2:29-42). The proclamation of the gospel was accompanied by signs and wonders through the power of the Holy Spirit which resulted in many conversions.

Preaching of the word in the early Church indicates how central Christ is and universality of the Church. Considering the happenings during this period, Boer observes that:

At Pentecost fundamental changes took place in the character and structure of the people of God:

a.	The New Testament universal Church replaced the strictly Israelites congregation as expressed in the temple and synagogue.

b.	The people of God ceased to be a national people and became an international, a universal community.

c.	The preacher replaced the priest, the pulpit replaced the alter and the Church's witness to the sacrifice of Christ, replaced the ceremonial sacrifices of animals...the Church has no capital city, no temple, no priest, no Alter, no holy land. It is at home in every nation; where it is, its Lord is fully present, and it worships God in many forms (18).

What Boer says here is the fulfillment of God's promise to Abraham in Genesis 12:3 "...and all people on earth will be blessed through you" (NIV). This is also in line with Stephen's speech (Acts7:1ff) before the Sanhedrininhis proclamation of the good news which he was arrested and charged for. Stephen began his speech as he took them back to the time when God called Abraham, followed by his descendants, to the coming of Jesus Christ, stating how God walked with the nation for the purpose of demonstrating His plan of salvation to mankind through Jesus Christ who is the head of the universal Church and the central message and the good news which the apostles preached during this period.

Stephen in his defense which he did by proclaiming the gospel which he was arrested for, also stated how the Prophets who preceded him were killed, and even Jesus Christ whom those Prophets predicted His coming. Stephen asked: "was there ever a Prophet your fathers did not persecute? They even killed those who predicted the coming of the Righteous One. And now you have betrayed and murdered Him" (Acts 7:52NIV), this led to his death as he was stoned to death.

After the death of Stephen, the apostles and the church were faced with serious persecution, in an effort to deter the preaching of the gospel but the more they were persecuted the more the gospel continue to spread, and God was adding to their number. In other words, persecution did not prevent the proclamation of the gospel and the apostles were ever ready to give up their lives for the sake of the gospel.

The Church continued to face persecution to the time of the early Church Fathers and the Reformers, but the emphasis in their preaching was Christ's death, burial, resurrection and exaltation(1Cor 15:3-5; Rom 1:3-4; 1Pet 3:18-22; Rev 15:3-4). The New Testament and the preaching of the early Church indicate how central Christ is, as far as preaching and teaching of the word of God is concerned.

Conclusion

To sum up the concept of preaching in the Old Testament, New Testament, and during the early Church, it is obvious that God uses different means to speak to His people at different times and in various occasions. The preaching of His word by those whom He usually assigns the responsibility both in the Old and in the New Testament and during the early Church, seeks to address the situation of the people and bring transformation in their lives. The instruments which God often use to get His message across were always conscious of the fact that their responsibility is to call the attention of the people to the truth of God's word and not to attract them to themselves.

The Cross of Christ has often been the central focus in the New Testament, and the Old Testament is foundational to all that Christ came and did even as what many prophets prophesied found their fulfillment in Him.The messengers of God were often faced with strong opposition and persecution but yet that did not prevent them from accomplishing their tasks as they were ever ready to risk their lives and die for the purpose of preaching the word and for the sake of the gospel.

CHAPTER THREE

SOCIO¬-POLITICAL HISTORY OF THE TEXT

Introduction

For "matters arising" from this exploratory study of the letter of Paul to Timothy, it is necessary to check out historical and contextual details. Basically, history is the study of

the past, in anticipation for a better future. Indeed 2 Timothy is an intriguing book to read through and study. It is observed that its intention was to encourage and guide Timothy as he led the Church in Ephesus. The book has a reoccurring theme,

About the book of 2 Timothy, which discusses the arguments regarding the authorship of the book, why Paul wrote to Timothy at this moment, and how significance the letter is to Timothy.

The second thing that this chapter addresses is the reason why Paul wrote to Timothy. The researcher deals with the exegetical analysis of the passage where the research topic emanated. Starting from 2 Timothy 4:1-2, analyzing the main clauses and phrases in the passage. It is an interaction as well, with scholars who have written books and commentaries on the passage.

The reason for the charge is the last part that the researcher handles in this chapter, which is found in 2 Timothy 4:3-5. It gives an exegetical analysis of the above passage and talks about the need of the charge to preach the word.

About the Book of 2 Timothy

The book of 2 Timothy is one of Paul's three epistles that are grouped together, commonly called Pastoral Epistles (1 Tim; 2 Tim and Tit). Second Timothy is also called prison epistle, because it was written when Paul was in prison at Rome about A.D 64-68. Scholars are divided about the authorship of these three letters. Some said that it is common knowledge that Paul, like other people, relied on their scribes for much of his letter writing. These anonymous scholars cite an example with the book of Romans, which Romans 16:22 affirm that someone else was the author not Paul. So is the same with 2 Timothy, where the nature of Paul's imprisonment might not have permitted him to get his writing materials to write a letter like this in prison. According to John MacArthur:

Many modernists critics delight in attacking the plain statements of the Scripture and, for no good reason, deny that Paul wrote the Pastoral Epistles (1, 2 Tim; Tit), ignoring the testimony of the letters themselves (1 Tim 1:1; 2 Tim 1:1; Tit 1:1)...these critics maintain that a devout follower of Paul wrote the Pastoral Epistles in second century (MacArthur, 1995: 1773).

Whosoever the authorship of this book and the Pastoral Epistles is said to be, it is generally accepted that Paul is the author, considering the testimony of the letters themselves in the above quoted passages.

However on the other hand, D.A. Carson and Douglas J Moo observe that the term Pastoral Epistles, "… is objected that the title is not completely appropriate because the letters are not taken up with pastoral duties…since they are directed to people with pastoral responsibility and with the task of appointing pastors, the expression is unobjectionable" (Carson and Moo, 2005: 554).

What Carson and Moo are saying here is that the objection about the designation of these three letters as Pastoral Epistles resulted due to the fact that the letters themselves only deal with issues that concern pastoral responsibility or directed to pastors but also address issues that are beneficial to those without such responsibility which is not debatable per say in these letters. Perhaps the letters are designated as Pastoral Epistles for the fact that they are written to someone with pastoral assignment for their benefit and the benefit of the Church as well.

What then is the reason for writing this epistle? There are several reasons that prompted the writing of this letter, of which one of them was to encourage and strengthen Timothy in the midst of fear of persecution. For Timothy was in danger of becoming weak spiritually. It was a serious concern to Paul, since Timothy needed to carry on Paul's work (cf. 2 Tim 2:2). MacArthur stresses that:

While there were no historical indications elsewhere in the New Testament as to why Paul was so concerned, there is evidence in the epistle itself from what he wrote…for example, in Paul's exhortation 'to stir up' his gift (1:6), to replace fear with power, love and a sound mind (1:7), to not be ashamed of Paul and the Lord, but willingly suffer for the gospel (1:8) and to hold onto the truth (1:13,14)…Paul calls him to…generally 'be strong'(2:1), the key exhortation of the first part of the letter, and to continue to 'preach the word' (4:2), the main admonition of the last part (1995: 1801-1802).

Paul wrote 2 Timothy closed to the time of his death. His situation has completely changed. He was at this time a prisoner in Rome about to be executed (2 Tim 4:6), after his first imprisonment and release. John Stott affirms that Paul: "was writing within weeks, perhaps even days of his martyrdom, according to a fairly reliable tradition he was beheaded on the Ostain way in Rome" (Stott, 1973:105).

For several reasons almost all of his companions have deserted him and Luke was the only apostle who stood by him to assist him (2 Tim 4:11). It was certainly a dark moment for Paul. Demas had forsaken him (2 Tim 4:10). His other associates at this moment were in distant places of ministry. False doctrines were spreading in the Church (2 Tim 2:17-18). Wiersbe says: "How Paul would have loved to be free to preach the word and defend the faith-but he was in prison at Rome. It was up to Timothy to get the job done"

(1981:146). Timothy needed encouragement in a time like this as he faces strong opposition and false prophets of his time who were deriving pleasure in preaching and teaching wrong doctrines. The Church at this point in Ephesus was actually facing intense persecution, which Homer Kent in his findings realized that: "After the burning of Rome in A.D. 64. At this time Nero wanted to stop criticisms against him and he blamed the Christians, and Christianity was made an illegal religion. Sometimes thereafter Paul was apprehended and faced certain death" (Kent, 1982:250). Timothy was to ensure sound preaching and teaching of the word of God, as he remains faithful to the proclamation of the gospel and ready to stand the test of his time no matter what, as Paul's ministry was coming to a close (2 Tim 4:6-8).

The Charge to Preach the Word: 2 Timothy 4:1-2

The passage under consideration clearly shows that there is a twofold charge with which Paul completes this letter, and each part of it is enforced by the consideration of events which are to come. The first group of commands is found in the second verse of the chapter; it is summed up largely in the clause "preach the word," and it is related to the difficult times predicted in the preceding chapter (2 Tim 3:1-9). The second part of this final charge is found in the fifth verse. It reaches its climax in the command, "fulfill thy ministry," and it is strengthened by the definite mention of the approaching death of the apostle (2 Tim 4:6-8). The first group of commands is especially related to the last half of the epistle, in which Paul has been urging Timothy to teach sound doctrines.

The first phrase to be considered before dealing with the subsequent clauses and phrases in this passage is the phrase "In the presence of God and of Christ Jesus" (2 Tim 4:1 NIV), and it is the ground of the charge to preach the word which Apostle Paul gives Timothy. Paul directs Timothy's attention to God and to Christ Jesus, in whose presence the charge is issued and received. God and Christ are witnesses of Timothy's responsibility.

"The presence of God and of Christ Jesus," (2 Tim 4:1 NIV) shows how one adverbial particle only in Greek, linking the two divine persons very closely together. In his affirmation of God the Father and Jesus Christ as one entity, Kenneth S. Wuest says that: "...God and the Lord Jesus Christ is a construction in Greek, which requires us to understand that the word 'God' and the names the 'Lord Jesus Christ' refer to the same person. The translation should read our God, even Christ Jesus; the word 'Lord' most appearing in the Greek text, (Wuest, 1952:152). The Lord Jesus Christ and the Father are always in agreement and in unity in their dealings with mankind in every aspect of life also, and in any responsibility entrusted to man. They are fully involved even in the responsibility of preaching the gospel which believers are saddled with. And by the Lord Jesus Christ every preacher and teacher of the word are going to be judged.

"Who will judge the living and the dead" (2 Tim 4:1 NIV). Christ is the judge of the living and the dead.The right and ability to judge all men belongs to God alone; but Christ clearly claimed it during His earthly ministry (Matt 7:21-23; John 5:25-30), because He and the Father are one (John10:30). "To judge" (krino) simply means to decide or to condemn, while "the living and the dead" clearly refers to those alive at His coming and the dead who have already died.

According to Philip H. Towner, "Paul however seems to teach that it is the believer's entire life that comes under the Lord's final scrutiny (1 Cor 4:2-5), and it does not appear to be a rubber-stamp affair. The fact of this impending review is given as strong motivation for Timothy to complete his ministry-faithfulness, now has a bearing on the outcome then" (Towner, 1994:203). As Timothy is been reminded that one day when his ministry is done, his work is going to be examined by the Lord Jesus Christ, Paul's admonition will certainly go a long way to motivate him in taking the task with all seriousness as he discharges his duty faithfully.

"And in view of his appearing and His kingdom" (2 Tim 4:1 NIV).This simply refers to his second coming in order to establish his kingdom. Gordon D. Fee stresses that: "...eschatological realities related to Christ being the judge of the living and the dead- Timothy should pay special heed to this final charge. After all, all of them he himself, the false teachers, and the people, will have to give a final account at Christ's appearing" (Fee, 1988:284). This manifestation of Christ is used of both the first coming (2 Tim 1:10) and the second coming (2 Tim 4:1, 8; Tit 2:13). Elsewhere the 'epiphany'is the appearance of Christ on earth (1 Tim 6:14). Here as in Titus 2:13, it is His return in glory, and is coupled with the kingdom in His thought, this might have given Paul greater importance of his exhortation to Timothy, which is very crucial as far as the charge to preach the word, and God's judgment are concerned.

"I give you this charge" (2 Tim 4:1 NIV) Most solemnly as with an oath Paul places timothy under oath to comply with the charge. It is to God and to His anointed Savior that Timothy (Paul, too, of course!) will have to render an account. If Timothy obeys, he will share in the glory of the 'epiphany' (appearance of Christ) but if he disobeys he will miss the glory and His reign.

Stott affirms that: "The same charge is laid upon the Church of every age. We have no liberty to invent our message, but only to communicate 'the word' which God has spoken and now committed to the Church as a sacred trust" (Stott, 1973:106). This charge is a special duty that requires total submission to Jesus Christ whom Timothy was charged in their presence and to whom everyone is going to give account.

"Preach" (2 Tim 4:2) NIV (kerusso), which simply means to 'proclaim aloud' which has to do with a delivery of a religious address publicly, especially to expound the gospel and to advocate. According to Edna Jane Travis:

The word; 'kerusso' is regularly translated "preach" and regard the preacher as a 'Herald' whose function is...to make aloud public proclamation... that has been given him by a superior. He must announce it in it completeness (Acts 20:27) and not alter it in any way, not add anything of his own or anything that is borrowed from another source, not subtract a particle. 'Herald' and not offer religious opinions, not philosophize, not argue(Travis, 2003:1865).

A herald is responsible to pass the exact message that has been given to him and he is usually very sensitive in order not to say what his superior did not ask him to say because he is fully aware of the implications and the consequences that will follow if he dare say what he was not asked to say. It is the same thing with a preacher of the gospel of Christ Jesus. He should present the message given to him and not his own message.

Wuest stresses that:

The preacher must present, not book reviews, not politics, not economics, not philosophy of life denying the Bible, and based upon unproven theories of science, but the word. The preacher as a Herald cannot choose his message. He is given a message to proclaim by his sovereign. If he will not proclaim that, let him step down from his exalted position (1952:154).

Therefore it is not a surprise to hear Paul charging Timothy with much emphasis to take the task of preaching the word very serious, because Timothy like any other person is vulnerable and not immune to those issues that Wuest points out and there is a tendency for him to compromise. He is expected to remain focus in his proclamation of the gospel and sensitive to any vices that may deter him from accomplishing his task.

"The word" (ho logos) is one of the titles of our Lord Jesus Christ found only in the writings of John in the New Testament (John 1:1-14; 1John 1:1; Rev 19:13). This title designates the divine nature of Christ. As the word, He was "in the beginning" and "became flesh." The word "was with God and was God," and was the creator of all things. In this charge which Paul gives to Timothy, "the word" refers to the written revelation of God which Timothy has been charged to preach. The word according to Don Fleming:

The writers of its several books were God's organs in communicating His will to men. It is His 'word,' because He speaks to us in its sacred pages. Whatever the inspired writers here declare to be true and binding upon us, God declares to be true and binding. This word is infallible because it is written under the guidance of the Holy Spirit, and therefore free from all error of fact or doctrine or precept. All saving knowledge is obtained from the word of God. In the case of adult it is an indispensable means of salvation, and it is efficacious thereunto by the gracious influence of the Holy Spirit... (Fleming, 1990:1203).

Following what Fleming says, it is clear that it was this written word by different authors that Paul was urging Timothy to preach. Perhaps during this period the New Testament was not yet written. The word is the most effective means He uses in bringing transformation in the lives of people. The word teaches, rebukes, corrects, trains, and encourages (2 Tim 3:16-17; 4:2). And this is what Timothy should do as he preaches the word.

"Be prepared" (2 Tim 4:2) in other words be urgent (ephistemi). It connotes the idea of standing by, being ready and being at hand. Timothy is to be constant in his duty of preaching the word. He was to be steadfast, and pressing urgent in the performance of his duty. He was also to embrace every opportunity of making known the gospel. Towner says that:

 Ministry means availability and preparedness...it brings to mind the doctor on call in the emergency room, or an obstetrician whose schedule must be determined by need, where readiness and availability might be the difference between life and death. It is the available Christian who will be able to seize the moment and win people for Christ and come to the aid of a struggling brothers or sisters in the church (1994:204).

The work of a preacher like that of a doctor is as crucial as life is to a man. It requires much attention, quantity and quality time. It demands that one should always be sensitive enough in order to maximize any opportunity that may come at any moment. Lack of readiness and preparedness of a preacher can cause deficiency and lack of productivity, as many opportunities may be missing as a result.

"In season and out of season" (2 Tim 4:2) This could mean when you feel inclined and when you do not and whether men are anxious to hear or not, as well as whether it is convenient or not. Putting the entire phrase together, "be prepared in season and out of season," Travis urges that: "we ought to think here not so much of the circumstances in which Timothy (or generally the preacher of the word) may be, but of the circumstances of the hearers; whether the time seems seasonable to thee or unseasonable for it...welcome

or not welcome, Timothy must ever be on the spot with the message from God"
(2003:1870).

In the light of what Travis is saying, is the fact that Paul did not promise Timothy that everything thing will be alright, neither was he trying to discourage him, instead he was preparing Timothy for the difficulties ahead so that when the time comes, such things will not be strange to him. And now that he has been told before hand, he will try to see that he prepares very well to face the challenges squarely as they come, and to ensure that nothing deter him from the ministry of preaching the word as he remains bold, courageous and focused; taking into consideration seriously these imperatives: correct, rebuke and encourage, these imperatives follow the first one that has been discussed already ("preach the word").

"Correct." (elegcho; It is closely related to the idea of "reproof" in 2 Timothy 3:16 and it is the same word used in Titus 1:9 ("convince"); also in 2 Timothy 2:15; 1 Timothy 5:20 ("rebuke"). In a sense Paul was simply telling Timothy that sin must be brought home to the sinner's consciousness in order that he may repent. In the same vein, heresies, moral transgressions and the like should be restricted.

To correct or correction rather, is a very difficult thing to do. Generally speaking correction is not something that people like. Many people hate correction, sometimes they like to correct instead of been corrected. However Timothy is charged to correct no matter the situation. What a difficult task! Imagine Timothy in the midst of those false teachers and wrong doctrines. Certainly it can only take the grace of God through the power of the Holy Spirit to do that.

"Rebuke" (epitimao). It connotes the idea of speaking seriously and warning in order to prevent an action or bring one to an end. A practical example is Jesus' rebuke to Peter who wanted to be a hindrance to His mission (Matt 16:22, 23).

In the New Testament the word is used to express a judgment of what is wrong, or contrary to one's will, and hence to admonish or reprove. It implies our conviction that there is something evil, or some fault in him who is rebuked…it implies authority or superiority, and means merely that a thing is wrong, and administers a rebuke for it, as if there were no doubt that it was wrong. (Travis, 2003: 1899).

This is another difficult responsibility as far as this imperative is concerned. Yet Timothy is to ensure that whoever errs or goes wrong is rebuked appropriately without fear or favor regardless of his status or position.

"Encourage" (parakaleo); the preacher must exhort. Here is the other side of the matter. No rebuke, no conviction should ever be such that it drives a man to despair and takes the heart and the hope out of him. Not also must men be rebuked without encouragement. It is the duty of Timothy as a preacher to rebuke and encourage, not rebuke without encouraging. Rebuke and encouragement must go together when dealing with a brother or sister. Therefore Paul charges Timothy to combine both in order not to do more harm than good to the person as it is the case, in many church organizations today.

How was Timothy expected to rebuke? "With great patience and careful instructions. "According to Travis, "'Be prepared… correct, rebuke, and encouraged' denote the manner of preaching the gospel while the phrase with great patience and careful instructions denote the method which Timothy must adopt…patient teaching is the most solid basis for ultimate success in the ministry" (2003:1905). As Timothy corrects, rebukes, and encourages patience is required, without being patient with the difficult people of his difficult and challenging time, he will not be able to accomplish the task given to him.

Exegesis of 2 Timothy 2:15The Greek version for 2 Timothy 2:15 says:Σπουδασον σεαυτον δοκιμον παραστησαι τω Θεω, εργατην ανεπαισχυντον, ορθοτομουντα τον λογον της αληθειας. The King James English Version says "Study to show thyself approved unto God, a workman that needeth not to be ashamed, rightly dividing the word of truth" (2 Timothy 2:15).This particular verse has three verbs in the Greek text: two of the verbs are in the aorist tense while one is in the present participle. The first verb in the aorist tense is σπουδασον, which, literally translated, to be diligent (KJV – study). The second verb, which is an infinitive (verbal noun), is παραστησαι, and may be translated as: to present. The last verb, which is a participle (verbal noun), is ορθοτομουντα, which is commonly translated 'rightly dividing.1.Σπουδασον. The above is aorist imperative and it is variously translated "be diligent," "be eager," "make every effort." The term according to Gunther usually implies both sustained effort and deep-rooted, serious, ethical motivation. He also adds that it could be translated "Make this your highest priority," or "Pour yourself into this task." "To study," it was translated "forward" (Gal. 2:10); "endeavoring" (Eph. 4:3); "endeavoured" (1 Thes. 2:17); "endeavour" (2 Pet. 1:15); "do . . . diligence" (2 Tim. 4:9, 21); "diligent" (Tit. 3:12,2 Pet 3:14); and "labour" (Heb. 4:11) . The King James Version here reads "Study to show [yourself] approved." This gloss has been criticized as an inaccurate translation of the verb σπουδαζω. Firstly, σπουδαζω according to Verbrugge is not restricted to mere study. It involves the whole person—heart, soul, and mind. Secondly, to translate this verb as "study" implies that the "Word of Truth" is a synonym for Scripture. Most likely, however, "Word of Truth" refers to the good news of Jesus Christ, which Paul had passed on to Timothy in oral instruction. . Therefore, since the word has changed in its meaning, it communicates something quite different from what Paul intended. Σπουδασον. Verb, aorist active imperative, second person singular, refers to Timothy, the primary recipient of the Epistle. This verb is in the imperative mood. Mood relates the verbal idea to the speaker's attitude or purported attitude. It presents something either as a fact or a possibility. Wenham establishes that there are four classifications of mood. The first is the indicative, which is the mood of assertion; second is the subjunctive, which is the mood of probability; third is the operative, which is the mood of possibility and the last is the imperative mood, which is the mood of intention. This particular verb is in the imperative mood making it a command. There are four basic uses of the imperative mood, namely: the cohortative, which makes a positive and direct command; the prohibitive, which makes a negative command; the entreaty, which expresses request rather than a direct command, and the permissive, which is the use of the third person imperative and needs the English auxiliary verb "let" to make its meaning clear. Σπουδασον can be safely classified as cohortative as this strongly suggests and expresses a positive and direct command. The tense of this particular verb is aorist. Aorist tense, basically, is indefinite as to time; when conveying abstract ideas, they express timeless truth. This peculiar tense to the Greek grammar was found to correspond closely to the English form often called "simple-present", which is really an English aorist, or indefinite form referring to a timeless fact or principle. According to Nordquist, in English grammar, the gnomic present is a verb in the present tense used to express a general truth without reference to time. Also called gnomic aspect and generic aspect. Casido suggests four kinds of the aorist tense, such as the ingressive, constative, gnomic, epistolary, for example, σπουδασον is of the gnomic kind, which states a general timeless fact or principle. This particular verb expresses both a direct command and a timeless general principle. The idea of gnomic aorist suggests a general principle. Here in this verse is a general and also a guiding principle. The most common way this verse is interpreted is to say that: if we study well, God approves of us and what we have done. It is more correctly interpreted that through our study, persevering and careful in work, hard-working, industrious, that which is done with carefulness, steadfastness, we prove to ourselves that we have been approved or accepted of God through the Lord Jesus Christ. 2. παραστησαι (to present). This is first aorist infinitive. An infinitive is a verbal noun. As a verb, its purpose is to express the goal of the verb to which it stands related. In this case, it expresses the goal of the main verb, Σπουδασον (give diligence). This infinitive is epexegetical, that is, it clarifies and completes the thought of the main verb. This infinitive answers the question, "be diligent to what?" The aorist tense reinforces the idea of it being epexegetical. Being a qualifier and modifier of the main verb, this word must therefore agree with the tense of the main verb, hence the aorist tense. If Christians are to be diligent about something, it must be in the realm of making themselves approved before God. Any practice that does not contribute to this intent must, by all means, be dismissed. To make ourselves approved of God is not a once-only task; it must be an earnest and continued effort. 3. ορθοτομουντα (rightly dividing). Accusative masculine, present participle of ορθοτομεω a late and rare compound (ορθοτομος, cutting straight, ορθος and τεμνω) here only in the New Testament. It occurs in Proverbs 3:6; 11:5 for making straight paths οδους with which compare Hebrews 12:13 and "the Way" in Acts 9:2. Robertson explains it to mean: plowing a straight furrow. The metaphor is that of a stone mason cutting the stones straight since τεμνω and ορθ ος are so used. Ορθοτομουντα (present participle). A participle is a verbal adjective. Its verbal function is to participate in the action of the main verb. Being in the present tense, it indicates action, which is contemporary with the action of the main verb. The main verb in this verse is Σπουδασον (be diligent) and Ορθοτομουντα (rightly dividing) is the participle. Hence, the idea being brought out is: as we diligently seek to be approved of God we must rightly divide the Word of Truth. In other words, the more we seek diligently God's approval the more we must be occupied in or with the rightly divided Truth. On the issue of finding God's approval, there is no substitute for the rightly dividing of the Word. No amount of Christian practice will gain God's approval apart from the right division of the Word of Truth. Hence, any practice whatever or however sincere and faithful it may be will only result in God's disapproval if not based on the principle of right division. To be approved of God may possibly require several and different ways and means, but what is most interesting in this passage is that the entire conceivable ways and means only one is mentioned, namely: the right dividing of the word of Truth. The reason seems obvious – our Christian practices or works are only the result of our knowledge of the word. In other words, we are not better than our theology. Hence, a knowledge based on the word not rightly divided will surely result in wrong practice. Therefore, to be a workman not needing to be ashamed is the result of the right division of the Word of Truth. Theological Implication for the Contemporary Church A church without theology is a church without God, as theology is about knowing who God is and what He has done for us which affects all of our beings, including relationships, goals, and the directions we take in life. A theology without a loving, sovereign God is simply not an option for the church or our daily faith, because we will replace Him with idols, or our own will! A Christian life without good doctrine behind it will be meaningless and shallow at best; erroneous and cultic at worst! Therefore, theology, that is good theology, is a logical system of truth that is rationally defused from what the Scriptures clearly teach. We are never to read in what is not there or just believe in something because it is what we grew up being taught, such an act is eisegesis. We are to be Bible-believing Christians who crave to put the Bible first-above all desires, feelings, or schemes of thought. Therefore, below are some selected points that reveal the implication of theology in the Church: Theology is the Knowledge and Application of Faith What you heard from me, keep as the pattern of sound teaching, with faith and love in Christ Jesus. Guard the good deposit that was entrusted to you-guard it with the help of the Holy Spirit who lives in us (2 Timothy 1:13-14 NIV).The passage above is a proof that theology is our boot camp and our duty is in application; it is the instrument with which God feeds our souls and grows our faith. The call of Theology is to continue to live in Christ, to be mentored and disciple so the truth of Christianity and solid doctrine gets inside of us, and then goes outside of us as we pass on the message of God to someone else. In other words, engaging the Word and Truth and passing it along-paying it forward (1 Cor. 11:2; 2 Thess. 3:6; 1 Tim. 4:6; 2 Tim. 3:16; Titus 2:1). The danger for the Christian is to sit in a pew, learn all she or he can, and then take comfort in that knowledge, never doing anything with it. The call is to know and be prepared by faith, to grow in spiritual maturity, to develop godly character, and to be infused by the Spirit and His resulting Fruit. Simply put, it is for this reason that Christ came. In the meantime, we partake in the building of His Kingdom with the bricks of our faith, each one interlocking with another. Theology is Attaining Spiritual MaturitySee to it that no one takes you captive through hollow and deceptive philosophy, which depends on human tradition and the elemental spiritual forces of this world rather than on Christ (Colossians 2:8).The Colossians had received the Gospel, but now they were diluting it with falsehoods, missing the main thing just as many churches, TV ministries, and so-called pastors do today. Oyetade calls this attitude 'religious abuse', which is causing psychological, spiritual and emotional damage suffered by members of authoritarian communities of faith whenever its spiritual authority is twisted by spiritual leaders to achieve a desired goal through unethical, cruel and damaging means. Theology has the theme of "paying it forward," meaning we receive a gift from God that is meant to be known and shared and passed on. We benefit from it and we get to continually use it, but we also get to show others so they can take it and pay and pass it on, and so forth. The reason why Paul used this metaphor in Colossians 2:8 is because the Colossians had become complacent and believed that I received Christ so I can rest in my laurels and do nothing with my faith now. Saved? Yes, perhaps. But, of what good are we in the kingdom when we do not learn and grow in the Lord? What good are we if we are not able to further the Gospel because we are disobedient to His Word? YOUNG PASTOR TIMOTHYA. Paul Exhorted Timothy to Study: - Paul recognized that an effective minister must continue to study the Word of God and the work of ministry. Paul admonished Timothy to "study to shew thyself approved unto God" (II Timothy 2:15). In other words, it would be his diligent study that would garner God's approval. It would be his continued study that would produce and maintain Timothy as an effective minister. The same is true of ministers today. Ministers who stop studying cannot take their congregation any further. The minister's failure to grow spiritually governs the potential growth of the congregation. An effective minister is knowledgeable in the Word of God, Christian theology, Christian spirituality, and pastoral care of all believers from young to old. In addition to the above tasks, the contemporary minister may wish to become proficient in finances, non-profit leadership, building maintenance, ethical conduct, and other legal matters. It is through knowledge and genuine care that ministers receive approval and fidelity from the congregation they serve.B. Seek Approval from God :- Not only does the minister look for approval, acceptance, and assurance from the congregation, but most important, the minister seeks approval from God. At the end of the day, what matters most is not a pleased congregation, but a God who is pleased with our ministry. This assertion does not mean that ministers are justified in abusing or neglecting a congregation because they are too busy "pleasing God." However, this does mean a happy congregation is not always a sure sign that a pastor is working with God's approval. The hearts of ministers await the day when they hear Jesus say, "Well done, thou good and faithful servant" (Matthew 25:21). We must all strive to please the Lord with all the responsibilities, gifting, and callings He has put into our hands.C. Rightly Divide the Word:- Ministers must seek to "rightly divide" the Word of truth. The words rightly divide represent the word orthotomeó in Greek. This verb is interesting because it is a compound verb—a verb formed by putting two words together. The first word is orthós, which is connected to the English word orthodoxy, meaning "right doctrine." Some people receive braces to straighten their teeth. The specialist who installs and cares for those with braces is called an orthodontist. Therefore, the range of orthós has to do with something being right and straight. The second word, temnō, means "to cut." Other translations use the words "rightly handling," "accurately handling," or "straightly cutting," for the word orthotomeó. If there is a "right way" to handle God's Word, there also must be a "wrong way" to use the Word of God. As fellow laborers studying God's Word, we must strive to use God's Word correctly."But we will devote ourselves . . . to the ministry of the word" (Acts 6.4). The matter of serving people with God's word is called the ministry of the word; the person who so serves is called a minister. "Ministry" points to the matter, while "minister" speaks of the person. The ministry of the word occupies an important place in the work of God. There are definite principles to be learned by those who preach the word of God and serve people with God's word.D. We Must Handle God's Word with Respect :- When visualizing the word workman, it is natural to think of the idea of tools. In the practice of ministry, ministers are working with the Word of God to accomplish the labor of ministry. A gifted workman does not only know about and understand the function of his tools, but he is also skilled in using his tools. Some of the tools we have at our disposal are historical and cultural resources, grammatical and literary resources, in addition to the experience and wisdom of other pastors and ministers. Sometimes the process of correctly interpreting God's Word is described using the words hermeneutics and exegesis. The Bible was written in distinctive historical settings, within unique cultures. In order to best understand the meaning of any given biblical text, interpreters should seek to unearth what that text may have meant to its original audience. Theologians sometimes refer to this concept as finding the stiz im leben, which is German for "setting in life." When we know the setting in life of the original audience, we can best understand what God is speaking to us through the Scriptures. The use of literary resources is also extremely important. Before drawing implications about the meaning of any given text, we should make sure we understand the English grammar of the text. If the grammar or language of the particular translation you may be using seems hard to understand, consulting other translations may bring clarity. Although the original languages are accessible through printed and electronic materials (e.g., concordances, lexicons, and dictionaries), some may struggle to adequately understand Hebrew and Greek, if not formally trained in their use. Finally Bible interpretation is meant to be performed in community. Because we have pastors and other ministers' active in our lives, we should consult them in our study. Nearly every New Testament book was originally written to groups of Christians. With this thought in mind, it is important to strive to study and interpret their meaning and applications in the context of community.II. FAITHFUL TO THE CALL Timothy was tasked by Paul multiple times to remain faithful to the call. In II Timothy, Paul encouraged Timothy to uphold the gospel that had been entrusted to him (II Timothy 1:14), to continue faithfully in it (II Timothy 3:14), to preach the Word at all times (II Timothy 4:2), and finally, to suffer for it if necessary (II Timothy 1:8; 2:3). Based on Timothy's previous history with Paul, it seems that he continued to remain faithful to the Word of God and His calling.A. Faithfully Use the Word of God In II Timothy 3:16, Paul affirmed that, "All scripture is given by inspiration of God." The word inspiration comes from the Greek word, theopneustos, which means "God breathed." This word is another compound word in Greek putting the noun for God, theós, and the verb pnéō, meaning to "breathe out." This definition implies that the Word of God flows from the very mouth of God. Believers should also notice that Paul cited examples that God's Word is profitable, or useful: "for reproof, for correction, for instruction in righteousness." Additionally in verse 15, Paul explained that the Scriptures "are able to make thee wise unto salvation through faith which is in Christ Jesus." This Scripture is good for rebuking, correcting, and training in righteous living. The Scriptures are also useful in giving us wisdom for salvation. Finally Paul explained in Romans 15:4 that the Scriptures were written for our learning: to give us hope and encourage us as we wait for the fulfillment of God's promises. The Scripture has a variety of functions for "a workman that needeth not to be ashamed" (II Timothy 2:15) to complete his ministerial task. All ministers should strive to use God's Word according to its usefulness. If ministers do not use the Word according to its usefulness, they are wrongly dividing (II Timothy 2:15) the Word of truth. For example, the Bible does make some scientific assertions; however, it is not a book of science. Additionally the Bible has insight into healthy human functioning; however, it is not primarily a guide for practicing medicine or counseling. We must use the Bible for what it is. To fail in this respect is to misuse and abuse the integrity of the Bible.B. We Must Study to Understand God's Word:- In the previous section, Romans 15:4 was cited to explain that the Scriptures were written for our learning. Here Paul made an important distinction. The Scriptures were written for us, but they were not written directly to us. For example, Paul's letter to Rome was written to a congregation located in the city of Rome in the first century. Though the Book of Romans is bursting with theological content that is for our benefit, in order to understand it in its original context, we must remember that Paul wrote the letter to the church at Rome. Since the Bible is written by human authors to human recipients in specific cultures, times, and places very different from our own, we must study God's Word with that reality in mind. Earlier we discussed how to respect God's Word. In order to fully respect God's Word, we must approach God's Word for what it is rather than for what we would have it to be. It is beyond doubt that God inspired the biblical writers (II Timothy 3:16, II Peter 1:21); however, it is also beyond doubt that the Bible was produced with human hands in unique cultures and situations. As we grow in our understanding of God's Word, we will develop a deeper respect for the Word and become more capable of using the Word effectively for His glory.C. To Know Jesus in His Fullness, We Should Be Diligent in Studying God's Word To increase the intimacy of our relationship with Jesus, we must be diligent in studying God's Word. In addition to the Bible being God's Word, the Bible also attests to someone else being the Word of God. John 1:1 declares, "In the beginning was the Word, and the Word was with God, and the Word was God." In verse 14, John wrote that "the Word was made flesh, and dwelt among us, (and we beheld his glory, the glory as of the only begotten of the Father,) full of grace and truth." Just as God spoke Creation into existence (Genesis 1:1–3), God's Word has creative power, just as the Word was made flesh. God's creative power, authority, and voice are now embodied in the person, work, and words of Jesus Christ.When we read, study, and meditate on the Bible, which was inspired by the Holy Spirit, we come into community with Jesus Christ—the Word of God that was made flesh. We access God's creative voice in His Word. When we put His Word into our minds and hearts, it creates new life within us. It is impossible to fully experience Jesus Christ apart from sharing community with Him through His Word. This study of the Word is a different discipline than worship, prayer, praise, or listening to preaching and teaching. We must be in His Word. When we are in His Word, we are where God has spoken and has chosen for His Words to dwell. Perhaps Charles Spurgeon, a renowned nineteenth-century British minister said it best: "Visit many good books, but live in the Bible" (www.goodreads.com).Good Theology is based on God's Word Brothers and sisters, stop thinking like children. In regard to evil be infants, but in your thinking be adults (1Corinthians 14:20 NIV). We need to be aware of bad practices and traditions formed from bad ideas - those without merit, thought, or scriptural guidance. The Pharisees were famous for making their own traditions then forcing and conniving so others would obey them, thus missing what God had actually intended. Jesus responded to them in Matthew 23 by judging the leaders, who beguiled the people and dishonoured God by their hypocrisy. He speaks to the multitude and to His disciples, saying, "The scribes and the Pharisees sit in Moses' seat." Being thus expositors of the law, they were to be obeyed in all that they said according to that law, although their own conduct was but hypocrisy. The point for us is to not make up traditions that remove or distract from His principles. We are to see the Church as His and us as the servants; we worship and placate Christ, lift Him up, and never allow our ways to become "front and centre". Thus, we must make sure and certain, as Paul urges, that our traditions are from Christ, and that they are true, mutually beneficial, and used to further His Gospel and Kingdom. It is incumbent on us to remember that we are never to separate theology from practice. Theology is the "who" and "why" that translates into the "do" and "be" of life. The question is, will we be dedicated to our Lord or to ourselves? Jesus answered, "It is written: 'Man shall not live on bread alone, but on every word that comes from the mouth of God'" (Matt.4:4 NIV). Hear, O Israel: The LORD our God, the LORD is one. Love the LORD your God with all your heart and with all your soul and with all your strength. These commandment that I give you today are to be on your hearts. Impress them on your children. Talk about them when you sit at home and when you walk along the road, when you lie down and when you get up. Tie them as symbols on your hands and bind them on your foreheads. Write them on the doorframes of your houses and on your gates (Deuteronomy 6:4-9 NIV). Therefore, in the words of Krejcir, theology good theology "is a logical system of truth that is rationally defused from what the Scriptures clearly teach. We are never to read in what is not there or just believe in something because it is what we grew up being taught. We begin as Bible-believing Christians who crave to put the Bible first-above all desires, feelings, or schemes of thought". Moreover, Marc Cortez identifies four ways theology is practical to everyday life of the Church. The first on his list is worship. He pointed out that theology is fundamentally about knowing God more deeply, which necessarily leads to both love and worship. In other words, falling more deeply in love with him while at the same time falling on our knees in awe before him. Therefore, knowledge, love, and worship are the inseparable triad of good theology. Worship is the business of humanity. We were created to glorify God by living as His image bearers in the world, and this is something that should characterize every minute of every day. And when God's people gather to worship Him together, they are doing the very thing for which they were created. Thus, if theology deepens worship, then theology is inherently practical—i.e. relevant to the everyday reality of being human. The second is Transformation: Marc Cortez also adds that if you are truly knowing God and being known by God, you cannot stay the same. You will be shaped by that experience. So, once again, we see that theology is inherently practical in the sense that it affects who you are and therefore how you live in the world. Theology remains practical in that it shapes us as the ones performing the practice.

The third is service: Theology plays the role of servant in the life of the church. One of its fundamental jobs is to help the church think well and carefully about how best to understand, articulate, and live out what it believes. Theology does not exist for itself, only for the Church. And in that sense, theology, as long as it remains faithful to its calling, must always be practical (i.e. inseparably related to the practice of the Church). Theology as servant will always be an eminently practical theology.   The fourth according to Marc Cortez is inquiry: If theology is an inquiry into who God is, and if God is as transcendent and mysterious as we believe Him to be, we should not be surprised by the fact that theology wrestles, at times, with questions that do not clearly relate to specific practices, but they are still part of the broader process of knowing God, which is eminently practical in the best sense of the word. He concluded by saying that if by "practical" we mean that theology should relate to the everyday lives of regular people, then absolutely yes! If theology is the attempt to know God more deeply, and if this means that theology at its best leads to deeper worship, greater personal transformation, and more effective ministry in the church, then theology is deeply practical even when wrestling with questions where it's not entirely obvious how they connect to everyday issues.

The Reason for the Charge 2 Timothy 4:3-5

The word "for" or "because" (gar) in verse 3 introduces the reason for preaching the gospel or the word rather. It points to something that will happen in the future. Paul declares "for the time will come." During this time, men will not "bear the truth. They will not endure sound teaching… but…gather…teachers to suit their own desires" (v3).

According to Fee:

It all has to do with their ears, which (in the Greek sentence) are mentioned twice. They suffer from peculiar pathological condition called itching ears an itch for novelty…though itching is relieved by the messages of the new false teachers. In fact what the people do is to stop their ears against the truth (Acts 7:57) and open them to any teacher who will relieve their tickle by scratching it (1988:285).

This is certainly going to be a serious confusion to those people and a serious trauma for Timothy as a minister in time like this. It is of course one of the reasons why Paul charges him before the time comes to prepare and help him stand firm so that he will not be surprised as he sees things happening in such a way, and to be able to know exactly what to do in a situation like that.

In the midst of all these challenges in a difficult time like this, Stott asked a very crucial question and made some comment:

How is Timothy to react to this? One might guess that such a desperate situation should silence him. If men cannot bear the truth and will not listen to it, surely the prudent course will be for him to hold his peace… but Paul reaches the opposite conclusion. For the third time he uses those two little monosyllable su de, 'but you' (5; cf. 3:10, 14). He repeats his call to Timothy to be different. He must not take his lead from the prevailing fashion of the day (1973:111).

These people "will turn their ears away from the truth," refers to the gospel (1 Tim 6:5; Tit 1:14; 2 Tim 2:18; 3:7-8 NIV). "They will turn aside to myths" (1 Tim 1:4:7; Titus 1:14 NIV). These final charges given to Timothy in this letter are similar to what he told or charged him about in 1Timothy 1:3-7. Paul was actually charging Timothy against the presence of false teachers and apostasy in the church, Timothy should have an undivided attention. At this point according to Towner:

The combined thought of deceitful and dangerous false teachers and weak Christians eager to be led astray turn Paul's thought back to the charge to Timothy. He must be different. And the difference is measured first in terms of balance. "Keep your head in all situations" is precisely what many believers in those churches were failing to do. As a result, they acted rashly, with muddled thinking, uncritically accepting the false doctrines. In contrast to the false teachers (who have written suffering right out of their manual...) and their followers, God's servant must be willing to endure hardship for the sake of the gospel...the major theme of this letter (1994:205).

For Timothy to be a different person, and to be able to win the hearts, and influence the believers, the people in Ephesus in particular, to also have a balance ministry, Paul in his charge in this epistle, further gave him four more imperative apart from the five already discussed above, but including the one that Towner pointed out. These four imperative also serve as more reasons for the charge Paul gave to Timothy. Timothy is not only to focus on preaching the word to people without doing anything to help him as a preacher of the word. Paul says to Timothy as he declares in verse five:

1.   "But keep your head in all situations." It is a contrast between Timothy, the people and their teachers looking at what he has already told him in the preceding verses (verses 3-4), and the conjunction "but" which contrasts verse 4 and 5. "Keep your head in all situations" suggests that Timothy must 'stay sober.' It is a call for Timothy to take proper care of himself as he remains focus. The people will go after anything because they have 'itching ears.' But Timothy must be alert not to give in as he struggles to stand the test of the time.

2.   "Endure hardship;" Paul reminded him of what he has already told him (2 Tim 1:8; 2:2; 3:12). As clearly stated earlier, it is in the same context of preaching the gospel.

3.   "Do the work of an evangelist;" The word "evangelist" which is a noun is also found in Ephesians 4:11 and Acts 21:8. What Paul says here is in conjunction with the imperative "preach the word" in verse 2 where the charge, began.

4.   "Discharge all the duties of your ministry." Having reached the climax of his own ministry and about to depart (4:6-8), Paul now urges Timothy to faithfully do all that is required of him especially now that the time is going to be terrible.

Conclusion

The exegesis and the discussion in this chapter show how preaching the word should be highly regarded by Timothy the recipient of this letter, and any persons that God has entrusted the responsibility. In verse 2, it is obvious that this verse answers four important questions, following the exegetical analysis. These questions which summarize the whole discussion in this chapter include: why preach? What to preach? When to preach it? How to preach it?

The coming of Jesus Christ to judge the world and to establish His kingdom serves as a motivation for the preaching of the word, hence the need to preach in order to combat false teachings and wide spread of heresies that lead to wrong application of the Scripture and godless living. The word and nothing but the word is to be properly preached and applied appropriately. It has authority and power to transform lives and encourages believers to live in view of the second coming of the Lord Jesus Christ as well as the power to bring unbelievers to His saving knowledge for the advancement of His kingdom here on earth. No matter the situation, the word of God must be preached at any available given opportunity without fear or favor, by those who are saddled with the responsibility.

Considering Paul's charge to Timothy to "preach the word," Timothy and any other true preachers of the word are expected to be bold and courageous enough to: "correct, rebuke, and encourage…" the sole aim should be to address current situations, and application to life. By so doing the preacher and the hearer will be able to stand firm and also watch against any false teachings that are not in conformity with the teachings of the Scripture, which turns people's attention to a different gospel that is not gospel at all.

As the preacher preaches, and as the hearers hear, it is expected that both should live by the message of the word in order to have the power to stand firm even in the midst of darkest moments in life and difficult situations as the case may be. Application of the word by both the preacher and the hearer will also go a long way in influencing the society for godly living and in advancing the kingdom of God, as those outside the faith (unbelievers) will be attracted to come to the faith in Christ Jesus, due to the lifestyle of the preacher and the hearers. Sound biblical preaching and teaching will also help to distinguish false preachers and teachers from those who are truly called and given the responsibility. The people will be able to discern whose teaching is to be accepted and believed and the teachings that should be rejected and discarded.

CHAPTER FOUR

THE RELEVANCE OF 2 TIMOTHY 4:1-5, TO THE CONTEMPORARY NIGERIAN CHURCH

Introduction

In this chapter, the researcher is discussing the relevance of the charge to preach the word to the contemporary Nigerian Church as the topic implies. The following sub-topics are going to be considered. Which include: the need to preach the word in the context of the Nigerian church, what are those things that prevent the preaching of the word, the implication of preaching the word and the implication of not preaching the word?

4.1   The Need to Preach the Word in the Context of the Nigerian Church

Going back a little bit to the discussion in chapter three, following the exegetical analysis of the text (2 Tim 4:1-5), it is very obvious that what Paul cautioned Timothy about and which also made him charge Timothy to ensure sound biblical preaching and teaching of God's word is what the contemporary Nigerian Church and the society today wrestle with. In 2 Timothy 3:1-5, Paul stresses that:

…there will be terrible times in the last days. People will be lovers of themselves, lovers of money, boastful, proud, abusive, disobedient to their parents, ungrateful, unholy… having the form of godliness but denying its power… In 4:3-4 Paul also makes it clear that …men will not put up with sound doctrine. Instead, to suit their own desires, they will gather around them a great number of teachers to say what their itching ears want to hear. They will turn their ears away from the truth and turn aside to myths (NIV).

These issues were the reasons and the needs for the charge to preach the word during Timothy's time; they are also the need and the reasons for preaching the word in this present age and many more, which this study cannot exhaust. They were the challenges of the church and the society then, and they are also what the church and the society is faced with today.

Possibly Paul did not have the present time in mind when he was writing to Timothy but it is very important to know that the issues of false teachings and terrible things have been in place since, as far as the preaching and teaching of the word of God is concerned. Right from the time of the prophets and priests in the Old Testament down to the New Testament, beginning with the ministry of the Lord Jesus Christ, the apostles and the early church fathers, to the present age. False prophets, false preachers and teachers have been in existence, that the devil has been using to advance his coast and to oppose anything good that is in accordance with God's will. So what the church is faced with today is not something strange. Gideon Yohanna Tambiyi observes that:

False teaching tends to spread more rapidly and faster than sound doctrines. Members easily adopt wrong teaching, careless and meaningless illustrations than the sound effort made by preachers and teachers of the word in the church…false teachers are busy looking for biblical illiterate group of Christians who will follow them, since they always want most followers they can rally. They busy themselves in search for material benefits from their members. Servant leadership as practiced by Jesus is never in their prosperity 'lexicography.' They use their members to get money. Today, the fastest means of making money is to start up a church. We have so-called pastors who start up new "mushroom churches" and they are making huge amount of money. They live in expensive mansions and have expensive cars. All these are the money collected and manipulated gifts received from the members (340).

This is very sad and a pity, that many things are taking the place of sound biblical preaching and teaching of God's word. Many churches have now substituted other things for the preaching of the word, because of the love of material things (of this world), their concern and their minds are on things that are temporal which can only last just in this life, instead of being concerned and seeking for things that are of eternal value that will last for eternity. Those things are not evil per say, but of a truth they become bad in the end because they replace the sound preaching and teaching of God's word. They encourage and make people to be earthly minded, instead of being heavenly minded.

These types of preachers and teachers, who are carried away by the things of the world and misleading people, are liars and deceivers like the prophets whom Yahweh through prophet Ezekiel declared:

...woe to the shepherds of Israel who only take care of themselves! Should not shepherds take care of the flock? You eat the curds, clothe yourselves with the wool and slaughter the choice animals, but you do not take care of the flock. You have not strengthened the weak or healed the sick or bound up the injured. You have not brought back the strays or searched for the lost. You have ruled them harshly and brutally... (Ezek 34:2-4 NIV).

Yahweh was strongly against those types of shepherds as He further declares in this same passage (Ezek 34:9). These shepherds were not serving or having the interest of the people at heart, but serving out of their selfish interest. Imagine what Yahweh might say to these kinds of preachers and teachers today, as He looks down and sees what is happening in the ministry and of course in the church today. In this regard, Wilbur O'Donovan stresses that: "the greatest need of the church today is for those who can correctly teach and explain the written word of God. The most important ministry of prophecy today is the ministry of correctly explaining the Bible" (285).

On the other hand, Jay E. Adams asserts that: "At the bottom of all problems of preaching and pastoral effort, there is always one basic deficiency: the deficiencies of pastor/teacher himself. Our churches will hear better preaching only when it is done by better preachers; the congregation will receive better shepherding only when it is done by better shepherds" (23). The church and the society are in a serious need of sound biblical preaching and teaching of God's word by preachers and teachers, who can stand for the truth, that can defend the truth, preach and teach the truth and nothing but the truth. Preachers and teachers who will take proper care of the flock entrusted to their care without lording it over them or taking advantage of them.

In the same vein, Janvier observes that:

Society needs politicians, doctors, and teachers but what it needs most is preachers. African can grow for the better and overcome its own problems when God raise up a new generation of preachers who are committed to Him and His word...Nigeria is producing thousands of graduates each year and our thinking is moving more philosophical on things around us. We need great preachers to help cope with the contemporary situation. Television, videos, debates, schools, speeches, and government policies will never replace the need for great preachers. Preaching achieves spiritual growth in people's lives that nothing else will accomplish (9).

The society is corrupt, people do no longer desire the truth of God's word, and error has become a serious pervasive disease. Much of the things people hear, watch, and read through the media etc are nothing but lies, particularly those things that concern the preaching of the word of God. It is not a story at all even as Ron Phillips mentions: "the spirit of antichrist is at work in our nation. This spirit denies the deity of Christ and stands against everything we believe in. These breeds lawlessness and breakdown of society" (135). Ever since John has already forewarned the believers about this spirit as he declares:

 Dear friends, do not believe every spirit, but test the spirits to see whether they are from God, because many false prophets have gone out in the World...every spirit that acknowledges that Jesus Christ has come in the flesh is from God, but every spirit that does not acknowledge Jesus is not from God. This is the spirit of antichrist, which you have heard is coming even now is already in the world (1 John 4:1-3 NIV).

s and will certainly be the cause and the motivator. There is always a cause to anything that happens whether good or bad. It is only the sound preaching and teaching of God's word that can enable people particularly believers to distinguish between the Spirit of God and that of antichrist, between false preachers and true preachers of the gospel.

There is a great need of preaching the word of God by preachers and teachers who are truly called by God in this generation. Correct teaching and preaching of God's word will certainly lead to appropriate application of God's word and godly living. It will also enable the preacher and the hearers to view and examine everything that happens in this crooked generation in the light of the Scripture. And also help them to stand strong and unshakeable without compromise even in the midst of those false teachers and wrong doctrines that are not in conformity with the teachings of the Scripture.

4.2   The Nature of Preaching in the Contemporary Nigerian Church

It has already been observed that in our contemporary Nigerian Church, sound preaching and teaching of God's word is at stake due to the increase of false preachers who roam about from place to place preaching and teaching wrong doctrines that lead people astray. They enrich themselves at the detriment of their followers. These types of false teachers and preachers are becoming richer and richer while their followers become poorer and poorer. Now the question here is, what actually prevents the sound preaching and teaching of the word, which will certainly go a long way in combating those heresies and reducing (if not eradicating) those vices that have become a disgrace and shame in the body of Christ, and as far as the true preaching and teaching of the word is concerned? The answer here is that there are many factors of which few of them are going to be highlighted and discussed.

Leadership struggle: Desire for leadership at all cost has been a serious disease that is eating the Nigerian Church and the society like cancer, as it affects the preachers and teachers' dedication and commitment to sound biblical preaching of the word. In most cases these pastors who struggle to be leaders at all cost devote much of their time in working out strategies, moving from one place to another as they campaign and seek for those who will support their quest and aspiration. This takes much of their time and attention away from their primary assignment which they have been called to do.

Adequate preparation and serious study of the word is no longer there, as such they often end up preaching and passing their own messages because they do not receive from God what to preach.

The messages of such preachers appears to be empty, full of selfish ambitions, greed, and materialism, which have no doubt replaced sound biblical preaching and teaching of God's word. For this reason it is observed by an anonymous author that "today there are dead pastors who are preaching dead messages on dead pulpits to dead people." This is due to lack of focus, dedication and commitment to one's primary assignment and to the guidance and lordship of the Holy Spirit. In conjunction with this, Chris Dariya points that:

The struggles for titles and leadership…have infiltrated our ranks and files as many of our pastors, struggle for licensing and ordination. Some enroll in school just to be able to obtain a degree in theology so as to be qualified into leadership positions in their districts and amongst the ECWA executive. While these positions are not bad in themselves, pastors must understand first and foremost our call is to preach and not run after such things that will make us lose focus in the ministry (16).

On the other hand, Zachariah Chinne also observes and cautions that:

The ministry through a seminary education does not qualify a person for the ordained ministry, nor does additional psychological testing and field experience. Naturally these may be valuable and even necessary for ministry, but none of them alone or in combination is sufficient. Unless the Lord calls, consecrates, and commissions one for ministry one has no business being there (33).

What Dariya and Chinne observed and caution pastors about is actually what motivate many pastors today to go to seminary for further studies and the young ones to join the ministry because they see others "making it" but passion and sound biblical preaching and teaching is not in their definition of ministry and their aspirations. This actually prevents and stands as a hindrance to preaching and teaching of God's word as expected, which is why Kenneth Prior stresses that: "Academic achievement can go to a person's head; especially it follows an earlier life in more humble circumstances. Those who seek academic distinction because of awareness that knowledge is power...must remember that it also puffs up...the motive behind the pursuit of academic degrees needs always to be examined" (137).

Other things that prevent the sound biblical preaching and teaching are: pride (which in most cases lead to seeking praise and honor from people that only God alone deserves), greed, and the love of money. These things can be summarized as materialism and the love of this world. Audu stresses that, "whenever a pastor in the field allows deceitful motives to creep into his heart, he ceases, from that time forward, to be stable. He loses his commitment to the commission and faces a journey of many crises and confusion in his life" (38). In a situation like this, imagine what could happen to the preaching and teaching of the word. If the preacher becomes unstable and confused due to those challenges, what will become of the followers who look up to him? This led E.M. Bounds to ask many crucial and spirit challenging questions:

Can ambition, that lusts after praise and place, preach the gospel of Him who made Himself of no reputation and took on Him the form of Servant? Can the proud, the vain, the egotistical preach the gospel of Him who was meek and lowly? Can the bad tempered, passionate, selfish, hard, worldly man preach the system which teems with long suffering, self-denial, tenderness, which imperatively demands separation from enmity and crucifixion to the world? Can the hireling official, heartless...preach the gospel which demands the shepherd to give his life for the sheep? Can the covetous man, who counts salary and money, preach the gospel till he has gleaned his heart and can say in the spirit of Christ and Paul in the words of Wesley: 'I count it dung and dross; I trample it under my feet; I (yet not I but the grace of God in me) esteem it just as the mire of the streets, I desire it not, I seek it not?' (18).

What bounds is saying here in a nutshell is that the sound biblical preaching and teaching of the word is not for those who seek human praise and honor but rather it is for the humble. It is not for the selfish and those who run after worldly things. It is not for those who see ministry as a job opportunity to create and amass wealth but for those who work sacrificially and trusting in God to meet their needs. Those that their affections are on heavenly things, those that see the things of this world as nothing but dung, and these are people who will be bold and courageous enough to correct rebuke and instruct regardless of the outcome

The church will be healthy spiritually and its members will not be carried away by any kind of false teachings, and it will never hold to a different gospel that is not gospel at all, if there are these types of preachers and teachers.

Therefore the need for preachers and teachers of the unadulterated word of God cannot be over-emphasized. The need for those who can stand the test of time and preach nothing but the truth, whether the condition is favorable or not whether pleasing or displeasing. Those who will be ready to lay down their lives for the sake of the gospel, not people like Demas who deserted Paul "because of the love of this world" (2 Tim 4:9) and Alexander who did Paul a great harm and whom Paul charges Timothy to be on his guard against him because he strongly opposed their message (2 Tim 4:14, 15).

Studying to preach to others and not to oneself first, is another factor that prevents sound biblical preaching. It is very sad to mention that in the ministry today, many whom God has entrusted with the responsibility do not care to devote much of their time to study the word in order to allow God to minister to them first in His own way, instead they devote little time and pay less attention to what God says to them in the Scripture. Many times when studying the word they are only thinking and concern about others and forgetting the fact that the Scripture also speaks to them. On the other hand, a good number of them do not even care to study at all, because they often allow so many things to take their time while neglecting their primary assignment of preaching the word.

The study and self-application of the word to many ministers is been taking for granted as many of their listeners on the pews often say that "we are tired of listening to sermons we want to see a sermon," which implies that we are tired of listening without seeing the application of what is being preached by the preacher to his own life. Many preachers are ignorant or take for granted, of the fact that it is one thing to preach and it is another thing to apply what is preached to one's life which is the most powerful sermon that one can ever preach. Preaching and teaching without self-application amount to nothing.

In his charge, Paul urges Timothy to study in order to show himself "as an approved workman who does not need to be ashamed and who correctly handles the word of truth" (2 Tim 2:15). This is in line with what Ezra did during his time in Israel. The Scripture says: "For Ezra has devoted himself to the study and observance of the law of the Lord, and to teaching its decrees and laws in Israel" (Ezra 7:10 NIV). This is a challenge and a good practical example and legacy to the preachers and teachers of the present age.

Another sad thing is that some study in order to bring glory to themselves as they desire to be exalted and become the most renowned "powerful men of God" that people highly esteem. In this case, Bounds warns and encourage that one should: "Study not to be a fine preacher...look simply unto Jesus for preaching food...avoid all controversy in preaching, talking, or writing; preach nothing down but the devil, and nothing up but Jesus Christ" (19).

In conjunction with what Bounds says above, Adams also observes that, "One great temptation for instance, is for the minister to read the Scriptures only in terms of sermons and ministry. Since he must preach to others, counsel with others...it is not hard for the minister to neglect the sort of reading that is calculated to penetrate his own heart and affect his life" (23).

What Bounds and Adams are saying is actually a temptation that every preacher and teacher should strive to overcome because that actually prevents sound biblical preaching that makes a great impact in their lives (as preachers and teachers) and in people's lives. In preaching and teaching, sin must be exposed in order to shame the devil, as righteousness and godly living should be encouraged in other to bring glory to God.

4.3   The Effects and Implications of Preaching in the Contemporary Nigerian Church

To talk about the implication of preaching the word on the health of the church, it is very crucial and important for the preacher and the people on the pews to know that the word of God cannot and will never make any impact on a person's life without the help of the Holy Spirit. There is need to depend on the power of the Holy Spirit for understanding, correct interpretation, and application of the word. Donald J. MacNair points out that: "to use the Bible faithfully in ministry, we must enunciate its truth. We must be convinced of its authoritative relevance to any situation. And we must spell out its implication for daily living and for the new problems we constantly face" (64). In other words, both the preacher and the listener should have the conviction that the Scripture is authoritative since it is the revelation of God (2 Pet 1:10-21; 2 Tim 3:16, 17), of which God Himself inspired its authors to write under the influence of the Holy Spirit through Him those who read, study, preach, and teach will have good understanding and good grasp of it for appropriate interpretation and application. Hence the need to depend on the power of the Holy Spirit, because of the vital role He plays.

Paul would not have charged Timothy to preach the word if it does not have any positive implication in the life of the church. The word if properly read, studied, preached and taught, results to establishment of a strong bible believing church, faith in Christ Jesus, the numerical and spiritual growth and health of the church, more understanding of who God is, what He did and what He does, and will enable believers to distinguish false teachings, and errors in order to hold unto sound biblical teachings without compromise.

Establishment of a strong Bible believing church: If there is anything that can bring about the establishment of a church that holds unto the truth very strongly and tenaciously, is the true teaching and preaching of the word. Usman Seth Nden asserts that:

Jesus preached the gospel of God and what came out of His preaching is the church (ecclesia). That shows that power is inherent in the word of God. If the church came into being by the proclaimed word of God and she is sustained by the word and the Spirit of God, then it follows that the primacy of the word of God to the life of the church and leaders of the church cannot be over-emphasized. Because we are what we are by the grace of God's word, it means that the word of God should permeate our thoughts, decisions and actions (82).

There would not have been anything like the church without the coming of the Lord Jesus Christ who spent most of His life in preaching and teaching before giving up His life on the cross. Since it is preaching and teaching of the word that brought about the establishment of the church, following Christ death and resurrection (the source of the gospel), it is the same preaching and teaching that sustains and guides the church in difficult moment and in everything. David Jackman also asserts that, "The Bible is the ultimate authority. The church stands upon the truth of God in the Scriptures, not upon its own traditions, not upon our reasoning process...but upon the word of God, upon the rock of the Scripture. That is the only foundation of which we can build securely. And Jesus Himself the living word is the message of the written word" (193).

This shows that if the Bible is taught and preached adequately and sincerely, the strength of the church will not be based on church traditions, or on anything else except on God's authoritative word, (the final authority of the church of Christ). And for Christians to be alive in Christ and with Christ, they must hold unto the teaching of the written word of God.

Teaching and preaching of the word lead to faith in Christ Jesus (Rom 10:17). It is through preaching and teaching of the word that people (unbelievers in particular), can come to the faith in Christ Jesus. It is the responsibility of believers (the church), to ensure that unbelievers are reached with the gospel by preaching and teaching of God's word which transforms people and delivers them from the dominion of the power and kingdom of darkness into the kingdom of light. Panya Baba observes that, "Many pastors tried to keep their church close to the biblical model as portrayed in Acts...the believers prayed together, learned together, praised God together, and had fellowship together. In that setting, "the Lord added to their number daily those who were being saved" (Acts 2:47) (238). If believers are united in Christ, having a common goal and living by the word, their lifestyles through the power of the word in them will certainly become a means of bringing others to the saving knowledge of Christ.

To the believers, the word rebukes, corrects, and instructs them whenever they err, in order to bring them back to the right track and encourage godly living (2 Tim 3:14-17). Jerry Vines and Jim Shaddix affirm that, "In a day which churchgoers are crying out for relevant application-oriented and need-direct messages...the word of God by nature is relevant, dynamic and effectual. It will take root and radically effect lives of those who receive it..." (Vines and Shaddix, 1999:56, 57). This is actually a motivation for the preachers and teachers of the word to always be prepared to preach and teach the word in such a way that it will be relevant to the listeners and speak to their needs.

Biblical preaching and teaching of God's word does not only lead to establishment of strong Bible believing church and faith in Christ Jesus, but also affects numerical, and spiritual health growth of the church. Kore affirms that, "Teaching the word of God has always led to the spiritual and numerical growth of the church of Jesus Christ. The only valid criterion for victory is to edify saints and help them to grow in the faith. The teaching ministry profits the flock" (Acts 20:20) (2013:83).

Loren Cunningham on the other hand, asked a thought provoking question about the word and tries to answer, "How can you describe that book which has foundational understanding for every human problem, steps to health and happiness, and building blocks for greatness in every part of society? That book is priceless. It is a real national treasure...it's a treasure that we need to put it to work, investing it in our lives and in those around us" (148).

It is a fact that preaching and teaching of the word leads to establishing the church strongly, (spiritually and numerically) to stand on the truth of God's word. But sometimes it also reduces the numerical growth, as some church members will not "put up with sound doctrines" (2 Tim 4:3), especially when it comes to rebuke and correction. Many church members because they hate rebuke and correction, will go away moving from one church to another, where nobody will talk about their sins and mistakes. They do not like preachers and teachers. David W. Bennet says, " warn the Christian community of impending difficulties (Acts 11:28; 21:10-11); who speak to encourage, strengthen, comfort, and instructs believers...they do not like preachers and teachers who bring people under personal conviction of sin..." (154).

Sound biblical preaching and teaching leads to more understanding of who God is, what He did and does in the lives of men. A person can never have such knowledge without reading, studying, and listening to the preaching and teaching of the word. No matter how eloquent a preacher or teacher is, if it is not the word of God that is been preached and taught, anything about God can never be known elsewhere even though nature reveals His glory also, but the word which is His written revelation does more. For what the Scripture reveals leads the believers to deeper and intimate relationship with their savior, and it serves as a source of their spiritual nourishment and growth. A. W. Tozer observes that:

For it is not mere words that nourish the soul, but God Himself, and unless and until the hearers find God in personal experience they are not the better for having heard the truth. The Bible is not an end to itself, but a means to bring men to an intimate and satisfying knowledge of God, that they may enter into Him, that they may delight in His presence, may taste and know the inner sweetness of the very God Himself in the core and center of their hearts (9).

It is only when the word is diligently and faithfully read, preached, and taught that a person can have such a wonderful knowledge of God as well as an awesome personal experience of Him.

Distinguishing between false teachings and errors in order to hold unto sound biblical teachings without compromise, is no doubt one of the implications that cannot be ignored in this study, because it is one of the things or issues Paul wrote and charged Timothy about, and which Timothy's preaching should also aim at, and the preachers and teachers of this present age. Clifford Hill says that; "The twentieth century has seen numerous messiahs and false prophets leading many astray with their deceptive teachings. Many cults have been formed by these prophets and counterfeits messiahs…" (281).

The contemporary society is faced with those types of false prophets and messiahs who have been misleading people. The only way to combat their false teachings and false prophecies is through preaching and teaching of God's word. This will enable believers to discern and distinguish between those who are truly called by God to do His work, and it will also help them to know the teachings that they will hold unto without compromise as they seek to please God and do His will.

4.4   The Implication of not preaching the Word

It is impossible to get people to submit to the authority of the Scripture in a church where the preaching and teaching of the word is neglected. MacArthur observes that:

There are plenty of gifted communicators in the modern evangelical movement, but today's sermons tend to be short, shallow, topical homilies that message people's egos and focus on fairly insipid subjects like human relationships, "successful" living, emotional issues, and other practical but worldly- and not definitely biblical-themes. These messages are lightweight and without substance, cheap and synthetic, leaving little more than an ephemeral impression on the minds of the hearers (118).

When the preachers fail in their responsibilities of preaching the word, there is that tendency of trying to please people and using human wisdom. They engage biblical Preaching and teaching of the word as if it's something out of fashion. It removes the lordship of Christ from the church. Gbile Akanni observes that: "One of the greatest challenges in the church today is how to get provision for ministry...the matter of who gives what, has discovered the nature of Christian service to the extent that the driving force behind several works, is not the desire to save souls, but the desire to get resources" (40). These things and many more have been causing a serious havoc in the church and they are the reasons behind the ministry of many so called men of God, which have replaced the sound teaching and preaching of God's word in many churches and the light of the church is growing dim.

In a church where teaching and preaching of God's word is neglected, the members will be more exposed to all kinds of deceptions, and they can easily be deceived and carried away by the strange wind of false teachers and prophets. Richard Ikechukwu. R. Diala says:

 Grieving of the behavior of so called men of God who instead of preaching the word of God faithfully, they fake the gospel...they dupe people. They are money making ventures. Somebody will charge about N50, 000 before "delivering another person"...it is also obvious that Anglican Church is now derailing. It is no more the question of the church but of going against the will of God. How can you marry two men or two women together? First of all, it is unnatural, it is abomination in any religion whether Christianity, Islam, Judaism etc. (13-14).

This is the situation of the church in Nigeria today. Many so called pastors and teachers of God's word have already drifted away from the true teachings of the word and are busy (looking for food) for their stomach and selfish ambitions. Many church members are being deceived on daily basis, because in their local assemblies true biblical teachings is taken for granted.

Today according to James Daane: "The pulpits are talk place, word cascade from it unto the pew, but little or nothing seems to happen. The lives of people in the congregation remain the same. The religious language of the pulpit may have a soothing effects on some troubled souls but it really changes nothing and the next Sunday the same troubled souls hear the same soothing idiom of piety" (17). These are places where many evangelical members go for solutions to their problems, because they look down on their pastors and sometimes because they do not want to be corrected and disciplined. Unfortunately for them, instead of having solutions to their problems they remain like that without any change and in most cases they compound their problems.

Another implication of not preaching the word is the fact that many preachers see themselves as super humans. They only preach to others and not to themselves. These types of preachers are arrogant in their preaching without any sense of guilt. In this case Poonen stresses that:

The body of Christ cannot be built by those who have a strong arrogant spirit, but only by men who have a humble gentle spirit. It is easy for an arrogant preacher to whip people in His sermons... Then he becomes like the servant Jesus spoke of, whom his master has appointed to give others their daily ration of food. But instead of giving them food he whipped them (Luke 12:45)! Unfortunately there is a lot of whipping that goes on from the pulpit in Christendom today. Whipping never leads anyone to a godly life, but only to feelings of condemnation, and to subservience to the preacher who whips him (46).

Eloquent preaching is another thing that Poonen also talks about which becomes a problem too, in regard to the preaching of the word in the church. He goes on to say that:

An eloquent preacher who is not poor in spirit...can only show us picture of wealth. He cannot make us actually wealthy... The church cannot be destroyed by adulterers and thieves-because these people are such obvious sinners that everyone can recognize as such. But the church can be destroyed by eloquent teachers who...who have no sense of their own need, and who yet preach about holiness (48).

For the fact that Paul charges Timothy to rebuke and correct (2Tim 4:2), that does not mean that preachers and teachers should use passages like this in the Scripture to whip their members forgetting the fact that they themselves are also not immune to what they correct and rebuke their members about. They are vulnerable to those things too. So correction, rebuke, and discipline   should be done with humility and they must accompany by encouragement "with great patience and careful instruction" (2 Tim 4: 2b).

Possibly the vices that Paul charges Timothy about in 2 Timothy 3:1-9; 4:3-4 which people will commit are as a result of this spirit of antichrist. The spirit of antichrist i

CHAPTER FIVE

SUMMARY, CONCLUSION, AND RECOMMENDATION

Summary

The first chapter of the research introduced the topic: "the charge to preach the word in 2 Timothy 4:1-5 and its implication on the health of the church." The background and the purpose of the research and other important issues about the study are also considered.

Chapter two was about literature review. The works of some selected Scholars who have written relevant materials on the topic under consideration have been reviewed. This gave the importance of preaching the word, the qualifications of those who are entrusted with the responsibility of preaching, and how God had used and how He uses people of different times to convey His message to His people. The aim is to help preachers and teachers of God's word to see how important and demanding the ministry of preaching and teaching is, so that they will become more committed and dedicated to the work and sensitive to the need of the hour.

The third chapter dealt with the exegesis of the text (2 Tim 4:1-5), where the research topic emanated. The charge to preach the word is something that the preachers of the word are expected to take with all seriousness, due to the fact that, the Lord who entrusted the responsibility to those concerned, will certainly demand an accountability of such noble task when He appears. The reasons for the charge also serve as an encouragement and motivation for preaching the word. God desires that the preaching and teaching of His word should gear towards helping His people to live godly lives in a godless and corrupt society. Biblical preaching and teaching if it is not taken for granted will definitely help God's people to live according to His will.

The fourth chapter is about the relevance of the study to the contemporary preachers and people. It is obvious that the ministry of preaching and teaching is seriously needed today, looking at the challenges of the present age, as many people do no longer care to live their lives here on earth in view of the coming kingdom, as such they derive pleasure in turning deaf ears to the sound teaching and preaching of the word. The positive implications of preaching and teaching of the word should motivate the preaching of the word. While the negative side of it should help the preachers and the teachers of the word to be alert, sensitive and courageous as they stand the test of time and remain focus without compromise no matter what.

Conclusion

This research discussed at length the charge to preach the word and the effect it has, as far as the spiritual health of the church is concerned. It is clear that sound biblical preaching and teaching is one of Paul's frequent themes in the Pastoral Epistles (1 Tim 1:10, 1 Tim 6:3; 2 Tim1:13; 2 Tim 4:2-3; Tit 1:9; 2:1) and it results in healthy Christian living. It is also obvious that sound biblical preaching and teaching is what many church members do not like, because they hate correction, rebuke, and discipline.

It is observed in this study that sound biblical preaching and teaching stands against selfish desires, and against anything that is in opposition to God's will which many preachers and teachers and their followers despise, but when it is carried out, it produces healthy Christianity. This study also shows that human heart in most cases, desires to turn away from God's truth and hold unto things that give temporary pleasure and satisfaction. However the preacher and teacher of the word are encouraged to remain focus in discharging their duties faithfully, whether people are ready to listen and heed to the warning of God's word or not, and also whether the condition is pleasing or displeasing.

Another important issue discussed and encouraged here, is total dependence on the Holy Spirit and surrendering one's life to the lordship of the Holy Spirit. For one cannot be effective, productive and fruitful in preaching and teaching without the help of the Holy Spirit.

The study further helped to understand that in this present age, false preachers and teachers are always increasing. A time that the ministry of preaching and teaching has become a lucrative business, which many people go into when other businesses crumble.

The preachers and teachers of God's word are made to understand that they are not immune to the trials and temptations of the time, most especially the desires of material things which have been causing many preachers and teachers to compromise. And sometimes they are tempted to preach and teach in favor of those they minister to, in order to obtain their favor as well. Hence the admonition to depend on Jesus Christ for the supply of their daily basic needs and to remain stable in preaching Christ, the living word who is revealed in the written word.

Recommendations

Having looked at the present age, how the preaching and teaching of God's word have been neglected and taken for granted, and how other things have replaced the preaching and teaching of God's word, the researcher deems it fit to research on Paul's charge to Timothy concerning the preaching of the word and its relevance to the contemporary church. For this reason, this work is recommended to preachers and teachers of God's, who are well known to the church and to the society as: men of God, pastors, reverends, evangelist, elders, deacons, Sunday school teachers, prophets, prophetess, canons, venerable, bishops, and a host of others who desire to preach and teach God's word.

The reason for recommending this work to those different categories of people or the ministers mentioned above is that God expect much from them. And they are the ones that people look up to in the church and in the society for direction, encouragement, advice, counseling, and for solutions to their problems.

The researcher desires that these categories of ministers should go through this work and see how they have been doing the ministry of teaching and preaching God's word and examine their work in the light of the Scripture in order to improve, where they are lacking. Perhaps they may not agree with some of the issues raised in this study, everyone is entitled to their opinion. But the word of the Lord should be the yardstick for measuring everything and the final authority to everything.

Furthermore, one will find in this study the admonition and the challenge to devote much time in reading and studying God's word in order to preach and teach it properly, for appropriate application. If a person does not spend adequate and quality time with God in preparing to teach or preach, anything can be preached and taught. Unless one receives from God what to preach or teach, there is every possibility of preaching and teaching to please people while displeasing God.

Another group that will find this research very helpful is DCC Chairmen and their Secretaries, General Superintendents, Bishops, and those who are saddled with the responsibility of administration. This will enable them to ensure that those pastors and teachers that are under them are doing their work properly and to see where they can encourage them to improve in areas they need improvement.

BIBLIOGRAPHY

Adams, Jay. E. Shepherding God's Flock: A Handbook on Pastoral Leadership. Grand Rapids, Michigan: Zondervan, 1980.

Adeleye, Bitrus Femi. Preachers of a Different Gospel. Step and Zondervan:HippoBooks.An imprint of Word Alive, ACTS 2011.

Akanni, Gbile. Tapping God's Resources for Life and Ministry.Gboko :Peace House Press, 2011.

Audu, Bitrus S. Introduction to Missionary Work. Lagos: Platinom publishers, 2002.

Baba, Panya.A vision Received, A vision Passed on.Bukuru: African Christian Textbooks, 2009.

Bennet, David W. Metaphors of Ministry. Grand Rapids, Michigan: Baker Books house, 1993.

Boer, Harry R. A short History of the early Church. Grand Rapids Michigan: Eerdmans Publishing Company, 1996.

Bounds, E. M. Power through prayer. Grand Rapids: Michigan. Baker Book House,   2010.

Calvin, Jean. Calvin Commentaries. Grand Rapids: Michigan, 1958.

Chinne, Zacharia. Men of Gold.Bukuru: Hamtul Publishers, 2013.

Cunningham, Loren. The Book that Transforms Nations: The power of the Bible to change any   Country.USA: Seattle YWAM Publishing, 2007.

Carson, D.A. and Moo Douglas J.An Introduction to the New Testament. Great Britain:
      Inter-   varsity Press, 2005.

Daane, James. Preaching with Confidence. Grand Rapids, Michigan: William B.E.
      Publishing   Company, 1980.

Fee, Gordon D. New International Bible Commentary: 1 and 2 Timothy, Titus.
Massachusetts: Hendrickson publishers, 1988.

Fleming, Don. Bridge Bible Directory: An A to Z of Biblical Information for the people of
today's world Bridge way Publication; Australia, 1990.

Hill, Clifford. Prophecy Past and Present Servant. Michigan: Ann Arbor, 1991.

Janvier, George. E. Biblical Preaching in Africa: A textbook for Christian Preachers. African
Christian Textbooks Bukuru, 2002.

Jackman, David. Understanding the Church. Great Britain: Kingsway Publications Ltd,
      1987.

Kent, Homer A. the Pastoral Epistles. Chicago: Moody Press, 1982.

Kore, Danfulani. The Truth for Healthy Churches.Bukuru: African Christian Textbooks, 2013.

Mac Arthur, John.The MacArthur New Testament Commentary 2Timothy.Chicago: moody
Press 1995.

MacArthur, John. Rediscovering Pastoral Ministry: Shaping Contemporary Ministry with
Biblical mandates. Dallas: Word Publishers, 1995.

MacNair, Donald J. The practice of a healthy church: Biblical strategies for vibrant church life and ministry. Phillipsburg: P&R Publishing Company, 1999.

Nden, Usman Seth. What the Church (Ecclesia) Exist For. Anglo Jos: Sele Printing and Publishing Press, 2005.

O'Donovan, Wilbur O. Biblical Christianity in African Perspective. Ilorin: Nigeria Evangelical Fellowship, 1992.

Phillips, Ron. Demons and Spiritual Warfare.Lake Mary, Florida: Charisma House, 2010.

Piper, John. The Supremacy of God in Preaching.Grand Rapids. Michigan: Baker Books, 2004.

Ponen, Zac. The New Covenant Servant.Soon House Publishers Jos, 1995.

Prior, Kenneth. Perils of Leadership. Downers Grove,Illinois: Inter-varsity Press, 1990.

Stott, John R. W. The Message of 2Timothy: Guard the Gospel. Leicester: intervarsity Press, 1973.

__________. With Greg Scharf.The Challenge of Preaching.Carlisle, Cumbria: Langham Preaching Resource, 2011.

Tambiyi, Gideon Yohanna. The African Church under fire: problems and prospects. Kaduna: Tubase Prints and Publishing, 2014.

Towner, Philip H. The IVP New Testament Commentary Series: 1-2 Timothy & Titus. Illinois: InterVarsity Press Downers Grove, 1994.

Tozar, A.W. The pursuit of God. USA: Christian Publications, Inc. 1993.

Vincent, Marvin R. Word Studies in the New Testament, Vol 1 Chicago: Moody Press, 1946.

Vines, Jerry &ShaddixJim.Power in the Pulpit: How to Prepare and Deliver Expository Sermons. Chicago: Moody Press, 1999.

Wuest, Kenneth S. The Pastoral Epistles in the Greek New Testament. Grand Rapids, Michigan: Moody Bible Institute, 1952.

______________. Wuest's word studies from the Greek New Testament. Grand Rapids: William B. Eerdmans Publishing Company, 1975.

Warren, Wiersbe W. Be Faithful it's always too soon to quit: New Testament Commentary on 1 and 2 Timothy, Titus, and Philemon. USA: Colarado Springs, 1981.

Wiley, H.O and Culbertson.1946. Introduction to Christian Theology. Kansas city, Missouri: Beacon Hill Press. Ferdinand, Kattenbusch. 1962. "Die Entstehung einer christlichen Theologie: Zur Geschichte der Ausdrücke theologia, theologein, theologos." Zeitschrift für Theologie und Kirche 11 161– 205. Murray, Michael J, and Michael Rea. 2012. "Philosophy and Christian Theology." Stanford Encyclopedia of Philosophy. August 9. Accessed November 9, 2017. https://plato.stanford.edu/entries/christiantheology-philosophy/Richard, Krejcir J. 2002. Why is Theology Important? October 2. Accessed October 17, 2017. http://www.churchleadership.org/apps/articles/default.asp?articleid=71446. Rivière, J. 1936. "Theologia." Revue des sciences religieuses 16 47–57. Edward, Farley. 1983. Theologia: The Fragmentation and Unity of Theological Education. Philadelphia: Fortress

Press. Wakefield, S. 1869. Christian Theology. New York: Hunt and Eaton. Aland, B., and et.al. 2007. The UBS Greek New Testament. Germany: Deutsche Biblegesellschaf.Tenney, M.C. 1973. A parsing guide to the Greek New Testament compiled by Nathan E.H. Scottdate: Herald press. Gunther, H. 1971. "σπουδαζω" in Theological dictionary New Testament. Grand Rapids: Wm.B. Eerdmans Publishing Company. Wommack, A. 2012. "Liberty Bible commentary." July 23. Accessed February 2, 2015. http://www.awmi.net/bible/2ti_02_15 .Verbrugge, V. D. 2000. "σπουδαζω" in New International dictionary of New Testament abridged edition. Grand Rapids: Zondervan Hornby, A.S. 2005. "Study" in Oxford learner's dictionary of current English seven edition. Oxford: University Press. p.1470. Wallace, D.B. 2012. "Crisis of the Word or A message to pastors and would-be pastors." July 23. Accessed October 17, 2017. http://bible.org/article/crisis-word-or-message-pastors-and- would-be-pastors-2-timothy-215. Tenney, M.C. 1973. A parsing guide to the Greek New Testament compiled by Nathan E.H. Scottdate: Herald press. Wenham, J.W. 1988. The element of New Testament Greek. New York: Cambridge University Press. Casido, B. 2012. A syntactical study of 2 Timothy 2:15. July 23. Accessed October 13, 2017. http://www.spiritualblessings.org/2tim.html.Nordquist, R. 2017 https://www.thoughtco.com/what-is-english-grammar1690579 March 23, 2017 accessed on Dec.02, 2017. Casido, B. 2012. A syntactical study of 2 Timothy 2:15. July 23. Oyetade, M.O. 2013. "An Exegetical Interpretation of the Greek Language in 2 Timothy 2:15 with Reference to σπουδαζω (Study)." Ilorin Journal of Linguistics, Literature & Culture. 3 101-111.Casido, B. 2012. A syntactical study of 2 Timothy 2:15. July 23. Robertson, A.T. 2006. Word Pictures in the New Testament. electronic database: Broadman Press. Casido, B. 2012. A syntactical study of 2 Timothy 2:15. July 23.Oyetade, M.O, 2013. "The Abuse of Pastoral Authority in some Churches in Nigeria Today" UMA Journal of Philosophy & Religious Studies 8 35-48.Richard, Krejcir J. 2002. Why is Theology Important? October 2. Accessed October 17, 2017. ttp://www.churchleadership.org/apps/articles/default.asp?articleid=71446. Krejcir,R.J. 2011. Francis A. Schaeffer Institute of Church Leadership Development www.churchleadership.org/ Krejcir J. 2002. Why is Theology Important? Cortez, Marc. 2014. "Does Theology Have to Be Practical?" Every Day Theology. October 2. Accessed November 10, 2017. http://marccortez.com/2014/10/02/theology-practical/.

Unpublished materials

Beattie, Charles. Lecture Note on prophetic Books. Jos: ECWA Theological Seminary, 2013.

Dewaay, Bob. "When a False Teacher calls America 'Israel.'" No page. Cited 20 July 2015.
Online: http://www.ciministry.org/commentary/issue.73.htm.

Diala, Richard Ikechukwu R. "Polygamy led to Exist of Anglican from Catholic Church
    of Nigerian Compass" Volume 1. (2009): 13, 14.

Footprints of Jesus (Magazine). An official publication of JETS Students: Volume 1.2
    March, 2015.

Singer, Dwight. Lecture Note on Pentateuch. Jos: ECWA Theological Seminary, 2004.

Travis, Edna Jane. Translators Workplace: Exegetical Helps on 2 Timothy (software).
Mexico: SIL International Impreso, 2003.

MIX
Papier aus verantwortungsvollen Quellen
Paper from responsible sources
FSC® C105338

Printed by Books on Demand GmbH, Norderstedt / Germany